OLD BALLADS

OLD BALLADS

Edited by

FRANK SIDGWICK

Editor of "Ballads and Poems illustrating English History,"
"Popular Ballads of the Olden Time," etc.

CAMBRIDGE :
at the University Press
1908

CAMBRIDGE UNIVERSITY PRESS
Cambridge, New York, Melbourne, Madrid, Cape Town,
Singapore, São Paulo, Delhi, Mexico City

Cambridge University Press
The Edinburgh Building, Cambridge CB2 8RU, UK

Published in the United States of America by Cambridge University Press, New York

www.cambridge.org
Information on this title: www.cambridge.org/9781107620155

© Cambridge University Press 1908

First published 1908
First paperback edition 2013

A catalogue record for this publication is available from the British Library

ISBN 978-1-107-62015-5 Paperback

PREFACE

NOTHING is more difficult in preparing a book of this kind than the selection of a title. In the present case the title is the simplest possible; but it needs a word of explanation. A companion volume, published last year, included certain of the popular ballads which deal with historical events; the present volume almost exhausts the rest of our national stock of ballads, in so far as they can be conscientiously adapted to school purposes. Many of the best have of necessity been omitted, for one reason or another; but enough good material is here, it is hoped, to stimulate interest in a form of literature which is only now beginning to be utilised for educational purposes. With such an object in view, an editor of popular ballads must be allowed powers of deletion and alteration which in a scientific work would be reprehensible, and I have therefore freely revised the texts; but I have not gone so far as to alter popular assonances into rhymes, nor have I changed the peculiarities of Scottish orthography, as the language is a vital part of these ballads. It would be impossible, for instance, to translate into equally effective English the last two lines of *The Twa Corbies*. In compensation, I have modernised four or five excellent long ballads from their seventeenth-century spelling in the Percy Folio MS.—*e.g. The Lord of Learne, The Heir of Linne, Will Stewart and John*, and *Thomas o' Pott*,—the two latter, I believe, for the first time.

The Introduction is an attempt to put before pupils in simple language an explanation of the fundamental difference between popular literature and the other kind. The teacher will easily be able to enlarge on the subject by suggesting parallels, from Homer to nursery rhymes. As to the ballads themselves, they are above all things intended to be learnt by heart; and I suggest that their strong dramatic qualities enable them to be *recited in dramatic form,* with narrator or spokesman, and a number of characters according to the personae of each ballad. Some of the longer ones have been divided into parts; or, rather, I have indicated a few points here and there at which the ballad-dramatist drops his curtain with the phrase " Let us now leave talking " of so-and-so, and raises it again with " Let us talk more " of some one else.

Not too much stress has been laid in the Notes on comparisons with ballads and tales in other languages; it is better for the pupil himself to evolve parallels from his own reading of so-called "fairy-tales," folk-tales or *Märchen.* Selections from Grimm or Perrault, and Dasent's *Tales from the Norse,* might well be read simultaneously with these ballads, in order to stimulate curiosity and research in this direction.

The textual notes are for the most part simply explanatory, and as a rule philology goes no further than a hint at derivatives still in common use.

F. S.

May, 1908.

CONTENTS

CONTENTS

INTRODUCTION.

BEFORE beginning to read the ballads contained in this book, it is necessary to understand quite clearly what a ballad *in the strict sense of the word* is; because the name has been applied, in one spelling or another, to many different things.

Derivation of the word Ballad.—It is derived from a late Latin word *ballare*, to dance; and it will be very important to remember this original meaning. Thence the Latin *ballatio*, and its derivatives *balada* in Provençal, and *balade* in early French, mean 'a song intended as the accompaniment to a dance.' Then it came to mean simply a song; and to the Elizabethans *ballates, ballades,* etc., merely signified any simple sentimental or romantic song of the day, set to a tune regularly repeated for each verse. Moreover the name was applied to other forms of composition; what we call the 'Song of Songs' was called the 'Ballet of Ballets of Solomon' in the Bishops' Bible of 1568; and above all, in the sixteenth and seventeenth centuries, a *ballad* or *ballet* meant a popular topical song, sung in simple metre to a well-known tune, celebrating or attacking some famous or notorious person. The idea of *song* in the word ballad remained current till late in the eighteenth century, and it was so used by such writers as Addison and Johnson. At the same time, however, the modern use of the word was beginning to come into existence; but it was usually necessary to qualify it with the adjective 'old.' 'The old ballads,' then, meant a number of songs, short, lively, written in verses usually of four lines each and in a simple metre, sung to popular tunes, and narrating a popular story. Many such songs it was the custom to publish as 'broadsides'—single sheets of paper with the verses printed only on one side, so that they could be used (as they often were) for pasting on the walls of rooms or houses. These broadsides were sold in the streets and in country towns and villages by professional singers and pedlars, who were accustomed first to advertise their ballads by singing them, and then to sell them for a penny per copy to the crowd they had attracted. But the term 'old ballads' today is not sufficient for students of literature, because it would imply the inclusion of all sorts of songs which at one time or another have been generally alluded to as 'ballads'; and therefore it is now customary to call them 'popular ballads' or 'traditional ballads.' So much for the history of the word. It is now necessary to learn exactly what is meant by a 'popular' or 'traditional' ballad.

Traditional Literature.—A baby learns a certain amount before it is able to read. As soon as it can talk, it reproduces words and phrases which it has heard spoken by others; and a little later stories are told to it from memory or are read to it out of a book. In other words, before the child acquires the power of reading for itself, its knowledge of language and its acquaintance with literature are obtained by 'oral tradition'—that is, by having those words, phrases, stories, etc., *handed on by word of mouth*. Of the two physical methods of transmitting language—speaking and writing—the child avails itself first of the *oral* method.

Now it is broadly true to say that the growth of the mind of a child resembles the growth of the mind of a people or nation. Those who are unable to read have the compensation of learning by heart, often more easily than those who can read; and this is true not only of primitive people in days before books were common, or before books existed at all, but also of illiterate people, such as are still to be found in many an English village. These people may be called 'unlettered,' but they cannot be called ignorant; and if they possess knowledge and yet cannot read, whence and how has their knowledge come? Obviously from other people, by 'oral tradition'—as in the case of the child.

The word 'Popular.'—We have been speaking of the 'people' above, both those who are 'primitive' in history and those who are 'primitive' in their knowledge. A moment's thought will show that the English adjective 'popular' is derived from the Latin *populus*, people; and its true meaning is 'that which belongs to, or appeals to, the people'; the derivation thence of its modern sense of 'that which is a favourite with every one' can easily be followed. Nowadays, when one speaks of a 'popular person,' one is understood to mean a person who is everybody's hero and favourite, and a 'popular song' is the song which every one knows. But in speaking here of the 'popular ballad,'

1—2

the older meaning must be applied—we mean 'the ballads that belong to the people.'

Popular or Traditional Ballads.—We can now translate this expression as follows:—'Simple narrative songs that belong to the people and are handed on by word of mouth.' But this definition demands further explanation.

In the first place, how can a song be said to 'belong to the people'? To understand this, we must go back in imagination to very early times, not forgetting that the word *ballad* contains the idea of *dancing*.

When people are gathered together to perform some labour, especially any piece of work where all must move together—for example, rowers at the oars of a galley, fishermen hauling in their nets, sailors round the capstan-bars, men reaping corn, women weaving at the loom or even spinning—it is natural and essentially human to accompany such rhythmic motions with the voice. When a mariner hauls on a rope, he says 'Heave-ho!' When one is in a swing, one is inclined to sing in time to the movement of the body. This innate desire, that the voice should accompany the moving limbs rhythmically, has always existed in the human race; and mankind gave vent to it in the earliest days, transferring to festivals— originally forms of worship derived from daily occupations—the song which accompanied those motions; hence came festal dance and song, intimately connected.

This is the beginning of *rhythm*, which is the parent of verse. Imagine a festival taking place in the childhood of the world; some community or clan are singing and dancing together joyously. Of what

are they to sing? We may suppose something has
happened in their clan—one of their number, let us
say, has slain a man belonging to another clan. They
make up a song, narrating this event; some one speaks
a line, another adds a second line, another a third, and
so on. When they have had enough of it, it stops.
Who is the author? Every one who has helped; the
song is made, not by one poet, but by the people; and
the song 'belongs to the people,' and it is a 'simple
narrative.'

The song has been made, but it is not yet 'traditional.' We must next suppose that the result is
satisfactory; those who have made it and those who
have heard it carry it in their memories. At the next
festival, or on any occasion which chances to recall it,
one of the clan begins to recite or sing the song again.
Is it likely that he should remember it exactly as it
was sung first? Enquiry would no doubt show that
most of those, who were present when it was made,
recollect different versions of the song; the main facts
of the story will be there in all versions, but neverthe-
less there will be differences between the song as
remembered by one man and as remembered by
another. And suppose there are ten different versions
of the same song current in one generation, how many
might there not be in the course of years? Against
this chance of variation, it is true, we must set the fact
that primitive memories are as a rule good and exact;
but they are not in practice good enough to transmit
traditional verse without variations.

Thus the popular ballad is born, and thus by oral
tradition it is distributed in ever-widening circles and
in numerous forms over an unlimited area. Remember-

ing our original supposition, that the birth of such ballads and popular stories took place in prehistoric times, we shall be able to understand more easily why it is that one can find ballads and folk-tales telling the same story in many different languages. *Nearly all the ballads in this book exist in other languages;* German, French, and especially Scandinavian, Norwegian, Swedish, and Danish. And we must not jump to the conclusion that therefore one of our ballads must be a translation of a ballad which happens to tell the same story in another language; it is doubtless nearer the truth to suppose that the ballad existed before the languages separated one from another.

Subject-matter of Traditional Ballads.—It is now obvious that any piece of history treated as a ballad stands a great chance of being corrupted by tradition[1] until it can scarcely be recognised for history at all; so that we find the earliest ballads to be those which are not historical; rather they narrate or illustrate phases of early civilisation. We might say they begin with mere jests and riddles; then, romantic tales are grafted thereon, success in winning a husband or a wife being made to depend on guessing or answering such riddles. This leads us to ballads of kinship and pure romance; next, ballads of superstition— miraculous transformations, witches, ghosts, fairies and other supernatural agencies. Legendary ballads are made out of popular tales from the classics or from sacred tradition, and some ballads (cf. *Thomas Rymer*) appear to have been fashioned about the fifteenth century out of the verse romances. As might be

[1] See my *Ballads and Poems illustrating English History*, Pitt Press Series, 1907.

expected, some of the latest ballads are those com-
posed about historical events so comparatively recent
that we can apply to them the test of independent
records; but even these we must admit as 'traditional'
on the strength of the fact that we find them existing
in the mouths of the people in more or less varying
versions.

The End of Traditional Ballads.—'Tradition dies
hard'; that is to say, it takes a long time for the
human race to forget traditional legends entirely. Con-
sider for a moment how much the memories of men
have been affected by the invention of printing in five
hundred years; and balance against that consideration
this other—that the mere fact of a piece of tradition,
story or verse, being printed, preserves it from entire
oblivion. Here is the dilemma; if you record in black
and white such a tradition (hitherto handed down
orally), you presumably prevent it from disappearing
altogether—but the mere fact that you do so record
it renders the chance of its *still* continuing in oral
tradition very small, because there is no use in tasking
the mind to remember things which are on record and
can therefore be re-learnt when necessary.

Traditional ballads, then, may be said to have
*begun to perish as soon as they began to be written
down or printed*. On the other hand, it is being proved
today that even in twentieth-century England it is still
possible to find old villagers, people of the humblest
and most illiterate class, who can sing certain old
English ballads, having learnt them orally from their
parents, who learnt them from theirs. Quite recently
a ballad has been taken down, from the singing of
Lincolnshire peasants, which narrates an event known

to have taken place in the fifteenth century; this ballad has survived in the memories of an illiterate class, without being written down, for four hundred years!

Methods of Corruption.—Traditional literature, of course, is far more liable to alteration and corruption than written or printed literature. In the following ballads many instances will be found, where something has obviously gone wrong; and while sometimes it is easy to put it right, it is just as often impossible to guess what the ballad originally said. Certain words, for example, fall out of use, and their meaning is forgotten; what do the ballad-singers do? In one case they will retain the word without understanding it—and this often leads to mis-pronunciation or alteration into a similar sound; in another case they will substitute for the old word the new word which has come into use—and this often means something more or less different. The schoolboy who had been told that the Equator was 'an imaginary line running round the earth' did not know what 'an imaginary line' was, but he remembered the *sound* of the words; and thus, when asked what the Equator was, replied, 'A menagerie lion running round the earth.' This illustrates one method of *corruption in oral tradition*, and in studying popular ballads we must always be prepared to find such corruptions.

Characteristics of Popular Ballads.—It will be convenient to note a few of the most prominent features of popular ballads—those which help to distinguish them from other kinds of verse.

In the first place the ballad is a narrative; it sets out to tell a story, and it tells it, by hook or by crook,

as shortly and economically as it can. Read the first
lines of a number of ballads, and you will see that they
waste no time in getting to business. As it starts without preface, so it ends without epilogue; the story is
seldom finished before the last verse. We shall see
that this feature can occasionally be made a test of the
genuineness of a ballad; where we find (say) a couple
of verses, drawing a moral at the end of a ballad, we
must suspect them of being an addition.

A ballad, economical of words as it is, often repeats
itself—sometimes a line, sometimes a verse, sometimes
a series of verses. Especially characteristic is what
is called 'incremental repetition'; that is, repetition
where some new feature is added each time.

Again, ballads have acquired a kind of vocabulary
and phraseology of their own, and are full of conventional expressions or 'commonplaces.' A few examples
will suffice. The ballad-town is 'Linne'; Linne sometimes has a mayor; the mayor has a daughter fair;
and she has 'twa marys' or two maids, 'to keep her
from thinking lang' (that is, from thinking the time
long, in days when two maids diverted you with their
conversation); if she wishes to send a message, there
was sure to be a 'bonny boy,' or a 'kitchen boy,' at
hand 'to run her errand soon'; if she finds it necessary
to stab herself or some other person, she always has a
'wee penknife' which 'hangs low down by her gair'
(that is, by the 'gair' or gore of her skirt, the gore
being the cloth cut to fit the side of the skirt). When
a man approaches a house, if there is no 'proud
porter' to be bribed 'with gold and fee,' the visitor
has to 'tirl at the pin' (rattle the latch). Boys who
go errands 'slack their shoes and run,' and when they

come to a river (usually the bridge is broken), they 'bend their bows and swim.'

These are only a few of the most frequent 'commonplaces' in ballads, but plenty of others equally picturesque and naïve will be found.

A conventional omission, also very common, is that of the speaker's name; a ballad will suddenly plunge into conversation without telling you who is supposed to be speaking. This, of course, is a natural consequence of the singing or recitation of ballads, for the narrator's voice can easily show the change of speaker dramatically; but it is not always easy or even possible to guess the speaker when reading a ballad for the first time.

These various characteristics will be found to be pointed out in the Notes as they occur.

Sources of the Texts.—We must now say something as to the sources whence we get the texts of our ballads. Firstly, there are printed sources—beginning with the 'broadsides' mentioned above; but these do not as a rule go back much before the seventeenth century, and even then they were usually re-written in a ·poor style for the broadside press. The printing of *collections* of ballads did not begin until more than a century later; but in 1765 came the first really important work on the subject.

This was called *Reliques of Ancient English Poetry*, collected by Thomas Percy, afterwards Bishop of Dromore; and in addition to the extraordinary effect the book produced at the time, 'Percy's *Reliques*' has remained popular ever since. Ballads had at no time lacked a champion; but towards the end of the eighteenth century English poetry had become highly artificial, and the *Reliques* may be said to have been the first step in the direction of assisting it back to simpler forms. The book strongly influenced Sir Walter Scott—who at the age of thirteen forgot his dinner, so entranced was he with his first perusal of the *Reliques*—Wordsworth, and Coleridge, all of whom played important parts subsequently in the revival of a simple and natural style of poetry.

But it is interesting to observe that Percy found it necessary to apologise for the roughnesses and crudities of the ballads, and not only to re-write and 'correct' these, 'the more obsolete poems,' but also to add 'little elegant pieces'—of Elizabethan verse, for instance—in order to make the *Reliques* acceptable. His ballads were printed from many sources; he copied some from collections of broadsides, and some were sent him, written down from tradition. But he possessed another and most valuable source of ballad-texts. This leads us to the *manuscript* sources.

In the first half of the seventeenth century, a man (who is thought to have been a Lancashire man, from his dialect and spelling) wrote down in a tall narrow manuscript book a very large number of traditional ballads, romances, and poems. We must recollect that at this date—roughly 1650—this man would probably be regarded as eccentric, for caring at all about old poetry; England was still full of glorious new poetry. His manuscript does indeed contain a few songs of his own day, but far the greater portion consists of old and traditional verse. We do not know whence he got it, but it was most probably written down from the recitations of people who knew the poems by heart.

About a hundred years later, this manuscript

volume belonged to a gentleman at whose house the
young Thomas Percy used to visit; the gentleman
did not value the book, and his servants used to light
fires with pages torn from it. Percy was already
interested in old poetry, and begged it from his friend.
Afterwards he used it to help him in making the
Reliques, though he altered its texts freely, and even
tore some pages out (including *King Estmere*) to send
to the printer of the *Reliques*. These pages have of
course disappeared, and we shall never know what was
written on them, or how much Percy altered their
contents to print in his book. But the manuscript,
torn and incomplete as it is, still remains one of the
ballad-collector's most valuable documents. After long
concealment in private hands, it is now safe in the
British Museum, where it can be seen any day exhibited in a case in the King's Library. Such is
Percy's 'Folio Manuscript.'

There are also other valuable manuscripts made by
collectors of ballads from tradition, chiefly Scottish;
but everything that is of value in these, as well as the
whole of the 'Percy Folio,' has now been printed, and
ballad-students who wish to find new texts must now
either ransack old books and manuscripts in the hopes
of finding something hitherto overlooked, or must go,
as they still may go with reasonable hope of success,
to the ultimate sources of all popular ballads, the
mouths and memories of the people.

OLD BALLADS

THE LORD OF LEARNE

[PART I]

It was the worthy lord of Learne,
　He was a lord of a high degree;
He had no more children but one son,
　He set him to school to learn courtesy.

Learning did so proceed with that child—
　I tell you all in verity—
He learnèd more upon one day
　Than other children did on three.

And then bespake the school-master,
　Unto the lord of Learne said he,　　　10
"I think thou be some stranger born,
　For the Holy Ghost remains with thee."

He said, "I am no stranger born,
　Forsooth, master, I tell it to thee,
It is a gift of Almighty God
　Which He hath given unto me."

The school-master turn'd him round about,
　His angry mind he thought to assuage,
For the child could answer him so quickly,
　And was of so tender year of age.　　　20

The child, he caused a steed to be brought,
  A golden bridle done him upon;
He took his leave of his schoolfellows,
  And home the child that he is gone.

And when he came before his father,
  He fell low down upon his knee,
"My blessing, father, I would ask,
  If Christ would grant you would give it me."

"Now God thee bless, my son and my heir,
  His servant in heaven that thou may be!   30
What tidings hast thou brought me, child,
  Thou art comen home so soon to me?"

"Good tidings, father, I have you brought,
  Good tidings I hope it is to me;
The book is not in all Scotland,
  But I can read it before your eye."

A joyèd man his father was,
  Even the worthy lord of Learne;
"Thou shalt go into France, my child,
  The speeches of all strange lands to learn."   40

But then bespake the child his mother—
  The lady of Learne and then was she—
Says, "Who must be his well-good guide,
  When he goes into that strange country?"

And then bespake that bonny child
  Until his father tenderly,
Says, "Father, I'll have the hend steward,
  For he hath been true to you and me."

The lady to counsel the steward did take,
  And counted down a hundred pounds there,   50
Says, "Steward, be true to my son and my heir,
  And I will give thee mickle mere."

"If I be not true to my master," he said,
  "Christ himself be not true to me!
If I be not true to my lord and master,
  An ill death that I may die!"

The lord of Learne did apparel his child
  With brooch, and ring, and many a thing;
The apparel he had his body upon,
  They say was worth a squire's living.   60

The parting of the young lord of Learne
  With his father, his mother, his fellows dear,
Would have made a man's heart for to change,
  If a Jew born that he were.

The wind did serve, and they did sail
  Over the sea into France land:
He used the child so hardly,
  He would let him have never a penny to spend.

And meat he would let the child have none,
  Nor money to buy none truly;   70
The boy was hungry and thirsty both;
  Alas! it was the more pity.

He laid him down to drink the water
  That was so low beneath the brim;
He was wont to have drunk both ale and wine,
  Then was fain of the water so thin.

And as he was drinking of the water
  That ran so low beneath the brim,
So ready was the false steward
  To drown the bonny boy therein.   80

"Have mercy on me, worthy steward!
  My life," he said, "lend it to me!
And all that I am heir upon,"
  Says, "I will give unto thee."

Mercy to him the steward did take,
  And pull'd the child out of the brim;
Ever alack! the more pity,
  He took his clothes even from him.

Says, "Do thou me off that velvet gown,
  The crimson hose beneath thy knee,   90
And do me off thy cordivant shoon
  Are buckled with the gold so free.

"Do thou me off thy satin doublet,
  Thy shirtband wrought with glistering gold,
And do me off thy golden chain
  About thy neck so many a fold.

"Do thou me off thy velvet hat
  With feather in that is so fine,
All unto thy silken shirt
  That's wrought with many a golden seam."   100

The child before him naked stood,
  With skin as white as lily flower;
For his worthy lord's beauty
  He might have been a lady's paramour.

He put upon him a leather coat,
   And breeches of the same beneath the knee,
And sent that bonny child him fro,
   Service for to crave, truly.

He pulled then forth a naked sword
   That hanged full low then by his side, 110
"Turn thy name, thou villain," he said,
   "Or else this sword shall be thy guide."

"What must be my name, worthy steward?
   I pray thee now tell it me."
"Thy name shall be poor Disaware,
   To tend sheep on a lonely lea."

The bonny child, he went him fro,
   And looked to himself truly,
Saw his apparel so simple upon;
   O Lord! he weepèd tenderly. 120

Unto a shepherd's house that child did go,
   And said, "Sir, God you save and see!
Do you not want a servant boy
   To tend your sheep on a lonely lea?"

"Where was thou born?" the shepherd said,
   "Where, my boy, or in what country?"
"Sir," he said, "I was born in fair Scotland
   That is so far beyond the sea."

"I have no child," the shepherd said,
   "My boy, thou'st tarry and dwell with me; 130
My living," he said, "and all my goods,
   I'll make thee heir of after me."

S. 2

And then bespake the shepherd's wife,
  To the lord of Learne thus did she say,
"Go thy way to our sheep," she said,
  "And tend them well both night and day."

It was a sore office, O Lord, for him
  That was a lord born of a great degree!
As he was tending his sheep alone,
  Neither sport nor play could he.   140

[PART II]

Let us leave talking of the lord of Learne,
  And let all such talking go;
Let us talk more of the false steward
  That caused the child all this woe.

He sold this lord of Learne his clothes
  For five hundred pounds to his pay there,
And bought himself a suit of apparel,
  Might well beseem a lord to wear.

When he that gorgeous apparel bought
  That did so finely his body upon,   150
He laughed the bonny child to scorn
  That was the bonny lord of Learne.

He laughed that bonny boy to scorn;
  Lord! pity it was to hear!
I have heard them say, and so have you too,
  That a man may buy gold too dear.

When that he had all that gorgeous apparel
  That did so finely his body upon,
He went a wooing to the duke's daughter of France,
  And called himself the lord of Learne.   160

The duke of France heard tell of this;
  To his place that worthy lord was come truly;
He entertain'd him with a quart of red Rhenish wine,
  Says, " Lord of Learne, thou art welcome to me!"

Then to supper that they were set,
  Lords and ladies in their degree;
The steward was set next the duke of France;
  An unseemly sight it was to see.

Then bespake the duke of France,
  Unto the lord of Learne said he there,   170
Says, " Lord of Learne, if thou'll marry my daughter,
  I'll mend thy living five hundred pounds a year."

Then bespake that lady fair,
  Answered her father so alone,
That she would be his married wife
  If he would make her lady of Learne.

Then hand in hand the steward her he took,
  And plight that lady his troth alone,
That she should be his married wife,
  And he would make her the lady of Learne.   180

Thus that night it was gone,
  The other day was come truly;
The lady would see the roe-buck run
  Up hills and dales and forest free.

Then she was ware of the young lord of Learne
  Tending sheep under a briar, truly;
And thus she called unto her maids,
  And held her hands up thus on high,
Says, " Fetch me yond shepherd's boy,
  I'll know why he doth mourn, truly."   190

When he came before that lady fair
  He fell down upon his knee;
He had been so well brought up
  He needed not to learn courtesy.

"Where wast thou born, thou bonny boy,
  Where or in what country?"
"Madam, I was born in fair Scotland,
  That is so far beyond the sea."

"What is thy name, thou bonny boy?
  I pray thee tell it unto me."   200
"My name," he says, "is poor Disaware,
  That tends sheep on a lonely lea."

"One thing thou must tell me, bonny boy,
  Which I must needs ask of thee:
Dost not thou know the young lord of Learne?
  He is come a-wooing into France to me."

"Yes, that I do, madam," he said;
  And then he wept most tenderly;
"The lord of Learne is a worthy lord,
  If he were at home in his own country."   210

"What ails thee to weep, my bonny boy?
  Tell me or ere I part thee fro."
"Nothing but for a friend, madam,
  That's dead from me many a year ago."

A loud laughter the lady laughed;
  O Lord, she smilèd wondrous high;
"I have dwelled in France since I was born;
  Such a shepherd's boy I did never see!

"Wilt thou not leave thy sheep, my child,
  And come unto service unto me? 220
And I will give thee meat and fee,
  And my chamberlain thou shalt be."

"Then I will leave my sheep, madam," he said,
  "And come into service unto thee;
If you will give me meat and fee,
  Your chamberlain that I may be."

When the lady came before her father,
  She fell low down upon her knee;
"Grant me, father," the lady said,
  "This boy my chamberlain to be." 230

"But O nay, nay," the duke did say,
  "So, my daughter, it may not be;
The lord that is come a-wooing to you
  Will be offended with you and me."

Then came down the false steward
  Which called himself the lord of Learne, truly:
When he looked that bonny boy upon,
  An angry man i-wis was he.

"Where was thou born, thou vagabond?
  Where?" he said, "and in what country?" 240
Says, "I was born in fair Scotland
  That is so far beyond the sea."

"What is thy name, thou vagabond?
  Have done quickly, and tell it to me."
"My name," he says, "is poor Disaware;
  I tend sheep on the lonely lea."
"Thou art a thief," the steward said,
  "And so in the end I will prove thee."

Then bespake the lady fair,
  "Peace, lord of Learne, I do pray thee;   250
For if no love you show this child,
  No favour can you have of me."

"Will you believe me, lady fair,
  When the truth I do tell ye?
At Aberdonie beyond the sea
  His father he robbed a hundred and three."

But then bespake the duke of France
  Unto the boy so tenderly,
Says, "Boy, if thou love horses well,
  My stable groom I will make thee."   260

And thus that that did pass upon
  Till the twelve months did draw to an end;
The boy applied his office so well,
  Every man became his friend.

[PART III]

He went forth early one morning
  To water a gelding at the water so free;
The gelding up, and with his head
  He hit the child above his eye.

"Woe be to thee, thou gelding!" he said,
  "And to the mare that foalèd thee!   270
Thou has stricken the lord of Learne
  A little tiny above the eye.

"First night I was born, a lord I was;
  An earl after my father doth die;
My father is the worthy lord of Learne;
  His child he hath no more but me;
He sent me over the sea with the false steward,
  And thus that he hath beguilèd me."

The lady was in her garden green,
   Walking with her maids, truly,   280
And heard the boy this mourning make,
   And went to weeping truly.

"Sing on thy song, thou stable groom,
   I pray thee do not let for me,
And as I am a true lady
   I will be true unto thee."

"But nay, now nay, madam!" he said,
   "So that it may not be,
I am ta'en sworn upon a book,
   And forsworn I will not be."   290

"Sing on thy song to thy gelding,
   And thou dost not sing to me;
And as I am a true lady
   I will ever be true unto thee."

He said, "Woe be to thee, gelding,
   And to the mare that foalèd thee!
For thou hast stricken the lord of Learne
   A little above mine eye.

"First night I was born, a lord I was;
   An earl after my father doth die;   300
My father is the good lord of Learne,
   And child he hath no other but me.
My father sent me over with the false steward,
   And thus that he hath beguilèd me.

"Woe be to the steward, lady," he said,
   "Woe be to him verily!
He hath been above this twelve months' day
   For to deceive both thee and me.

"If you do not my counsel keep
  That I have told you with good intent,   310
And if you do it not well keep,
  Farewell! my life is at an end."

"I will be true to thee, lord of Learne,
  Or else Christ be not so unto me;
And as I am a true lady,
  I'll never marry none but thee!"

She sent in for her father, the duke,
  In all the speed that e'er might be;
"Put off my wedding, father," she said,
  "For the love of God, these months three.   320

"Sick I am," the lady said,
  "O sick, and very like to die!
Put off my wedding, father duke,
  For the love of God, these months three."

The duke of France put off this wedding
  Of the steward and the lady, months three;
For the lady sick she was,
  Sick, sick, and like to die.

She wrote a letter with her own hand,
  In all the speed that ever might be;   330
She sent over into Scotland
  That is so far beyond the sea.

When the messenger came before the old lord of
    Learne,
  He kneelèd low down on his knee,
And he delivered the letter unto him
  In all the speed that ever might be.

First look he looked the letter upon,
  Lo! he wept full bitterly;
The second look he looked it upon,
  Said, "False steward! woe be to thee!"   340

When the lady of Learne these tidings heard,
  O Lord! she wept so bitterly:
"I told you of this, now, good my lord,
  When I sent my child into that wild country."

"Peace, lady of Learne," the lord did say,
  "For Christ his love I do pray thee;
And as I am a Christian man,
  Wroken upon him that I will be."

He wrote a letter with his own hand
  In all the speed that e'er might be;   350
He sent it into the lords in Scotland
  That were born of a great degree.

He sent for lords, he sent for knights,
  The best that were in the country,
To go with him into the land of France,
  To seek his son in that strange country.

The wind was good, and they did sail,
  Five hundred men into France land,
There to seek that bonny boy
  That was the worthy lord of Learne.   360

They sought the country through and through,
  So far to the duke's place of France land:
There they were ware of that bonny boy
  Standing with a porter's staff in his hand.

Then the worshipful they did bow,
　The serving-men fell on their knee,
They cast their hats up into the air
　For joy that boy that they did see.

The lord of Learne, then he light down,
　And kissed his child both cheek and chin,　370
And said, "God bless thee, my son and my heir,
　The bliss of heaven that thou may win!"

[PART IV]

The false steward and the duke of France
　Were in a castle top truly:
"What fools are yond," says the false steward,
　"To the porter makes so low courtesy?"

Then bespake the duke of France,
　Calling my lord of Learne truly,
He said, "I doubt the day be come
　That either you or I must die."　380

They set the castle round about,
　A swallow could not have flown away;
And there they took the false steward
　That the lord of Learne did betray.

And when they had taken the false steward,
　He fell low down upon his knee,
And craved mercy of the lord of Learne
　For the villainous deed he had done, truly.

"Thou shalt have mercy," said the lord of Learne,
　"Thou vile traitor! I tell to thee,　390
As the laws of the realm they will thee bear,
　Whether it be for thee to live or die."

A quest of lords that there was chosen
  To go upon his death, truly:
There they judged the false steward,
  Whether he was guilty, and for to die.

The foreman of the jury, he came in;
  He spake his words full loud and high:
Said, "Make thee ready, thou false steward,
  For now thy death it draws full nigh!"   400

Said he, "If my death it doth draw nigh,
  God forgive me all I have done amiss!
Where is that lady I have loved so long,
  Before my death to give me a kiss?"

"Away, thou traitor!" the lady said,
  "Avoid out of my company!
For thy vile treason thou hast wrought,
  Thou had need to cry to God for mercy."

First they took him and hanged him half,
  And let him down before he was dead,   410
And quartered him in quarters many,
  And sod him in a boiling lead.

And then they took him out again,
  And cutten all his joints in sunder,
And burnt him eke upon a hill;
  I-wis they did him curstly cumber.

A loud laughter the lady laughed;
  O Lord! she smilèd merrily;
She said, "I may praise my heavenly King,
  That ever I seen this vile traitor die."   420

Then bespake the duke of France,
  Unto the right lord of Learne said he there,
Says, "Lord of Learne, if thou wilt marry my
    daughter,
  I'll mend thy living five hundred pounds a year."

But then bespake that bonny boy,
  And answered the duke quickly,
"I had rather marry your daughter with a ring
    of gold,
  Than all the gold that e'er I blinked on with
    mine eye."

But then bespake the old lord of Learne,
  To the duke of France thus he did say,   430
"Seeing our children do so well agree,
  They shall be married ere we go away."

The lady of Learne, she was for sent
  Throughout Scotland so speedily,
To see these two children set up
  In their seats of gold full royally.

YOUNG BEKIE

Young Bekie was as brave a knight
  As ever sail'd the sea;
An' he's done him to the court of France,
  To serve for meat and fee.

He had nae been i' the court of France
  A twelvemonth nor sae long,
Till he fell in love with the king's daughter,
  An' was thrown in prison strong.

The king he had but ae daughter,
 Burd Isbel was her name;   10
An' she has to the prison-house gane,
 To hear the prisoner's mane.

"O gin a lady would borrow me,
 At her stirrup-foot I would run;
Or gin a widow would borrow me,
 I would swear to be her son.

"Or gin a virgin would borrow me,
 I would wed her wi' a ring;
I'd gie her ha's, I'd gie her bowers,
 The bonny tow'rs o' Linne."   20

O barefoot, barefoot gaed she but,
 An' barefoot came she ben;
It was no for want o' hose an' shoon,
 Nor time to put them on;

But a' for fear that her father dear,
 Had heard her making din:
She's stown the keys o' the prison-house dor,
 An' latten the prisoner gang.

O whan she saw him, Young Bekie,
 Her heart was wondrous sair!   30
For the mice but an' the bold rottons
 Had eaten his yallow hair.

She's gi'en him a shaver for his beard,
 A comber till his hair,
Five hunder pound in his pocket,
 To spen', and nae to spair.

She 's gi'en him a steed was good in need,
  An' a saddle o' royal bone,
A leash o' hounds o' ae litter,
  An' Hector callèd one.   40

Atween this twa a vow was made,
  'Twas made full solemnly,
That or three years was come and gane,
  Well married they should be.

He had nae been in 's ain country
  A twelvemonth till an end,
Till he 's forced to marry a duke's daughter,
  Or then lose a' his land.

"Ohon, alas!" says Young Bekie,
  "I know not what to dee;   50
For I canno win to Burd Isbel,
  And she kensnae to come to me."

O it fell once upon a day
  Burd Isbel fell asleep,
An' up it starts the Billy Blin,
  An' stood at her bed-feet.

"O waken, waken, Burd Isbel,
  How can you sleep so soun',
Whan this is Bekie's wedding day,
  An' the marriage gain' on?   60

"Ye do ye to your mither's bow'r,
  Think neither sin nor shame;
An' ye tak' twa o' your mither's marys,
  To keep ye frae thinking lang.

"Ye dress yoursel' in the red scarlet,
    An' your marys in dainty green,
An' ye pit girdles about your middles
    Would buy an earldome.

"O ye gang down by yon sea-side,
    An' down by yon sea-stran';   70
Sae bonny will the Hollans boats
    Come rowin' till your han'.

"Ye set your milk-white foot aboard,
    Cry, Hail ye, Domine!
An' I shall be the steerer o't,
    To row you o'er the sea."

She's ta'en her till her mither's bow'r,
    Thought neither sin nor shame,
An' she took twa o' her mither's marys,
    To keep her frae thinking lang.   80

She dress'd hersel' i' the red scarlet,
    Her marys i' dainty green,
And they pat girdles about their middles
    Would buy an earldome.

An' they gid down by yon sea-side,
    An' down by yon sea-stran';
Sae bonny did the Hollan' boats
    Come rowin' to their han'.

She set her milk-white foot on board,
    Cried "Hail ye, Domine!"   90
An' the Billy Blin was the steerer o't,
    To row her o'er the sea.

Whan she came to Young Bekie's gate,
  She heard the music play;
Sae well she kent frae a' she heard,
  It was his wedding day.

She's pitten her han' in her pocket,
  Gi'n the porter guineas three;
"Hae, tak' ye that, ye proud porter,
  Bid the bride-groom speak to me."   100

O whan that he cam up the stair,
  He fell low down on his knee:
He hail'd the king, an' he hail'd the queen,
  An' he hail'd him, Young Bekie.

"O I've been porter at your gates
  This thirty years an' three;
But there's three ladies at them now,
  Their like I never did see.

"There's ane o' them dress'd in red scarlet,
  And twa in dainty green,   110
An' they hae girdles about their middles
  Would buy an earldome."

Then out it spake the bierly bride,
  Was a' goud to the chin:
"Gin she be braw without," she says,
  "We's be as braw within."

Then up it starts him, Young Bekie,
  An' the tears was in his ee:
"I'll lay my life it's Burd Isbel,
  Come o'er the sea to me."   120

O quickly ran he down the stair,
   An' when he saw 'twas she,
He kindly took her in his arms,
   And kiss'd her tenderly.

"O hae ye forgotten, Young Bekie,
   The vow ye made to me,
Whan I took ye out o' the prison strong
   Whan ye was condemn'd to die?

"I gae you a steed was good in need,
   An' a saddle o' royal bone,   130
A leash o' hounds o' ae litter,
   An' Hector callèd one."

It was well kent what the lady said,
   That it wasnae a lee,
For at ilka word the lady spake,
   The hound fell at her knee.

"Tak hame, tak hame your daughter dear,
   A blessing gae her wi',
For I maun marry my Burd Isbel,
   That 's come o'er the sea to me."   140

"Is this the custom o' your house,
   Or the fashion o' your lan',
To marry a maid in a May mornin',
   An' send her back at even?"

THE TWA SISTERS OF BINNORIE

There were twa sisters sat in a bour,
  Binnorie, O Binnorie !
There came a knight to be their wooer,
  By the bonny mill-dams o' Binnorie.

He courted the eldest wi' glove and ring,
  Binnorie, O Binnorie !
But he lo'ed the youngest aboon a' thing,
  By the bonny mill-dams o' Binnorie.

He courted the eldest with brooch and knife,
  Binnorie, O Binnorie !   10
But he lo'ed the youngest aboon his life,
  By the bonny mill-dams o' Binnorie.

The eldest she was vexèd sair,
  Binnorie, O Binnorie !
And sair envìed her sister fair,
  By the bonny mill-dams o' Binnorie.

The eldest said to the youngest ane,
  Binnorie, O Binnorie !
"Will ye go and see our father's ships come in?"
  By the bonny mill-dams o' Binnorie.   20

She's ta'en her by the lily hand,
  Binnorie, O Binnorie !
And led her down to the river-strand,
  By the bonny mill-dams o' Binnorie.

The youngest stude upon a stane,
  Binnorie, O Binnorie!
The eldest came and push'd her in,
  By the bonny mill-dams o' Binnorie.

She took her by the middle sma',
  Binnorie, O Binnorie!   30
And dashed her bonny back to the jaw,
  By the bonny mill-dams o' Binnorie.

" O sister, sister, reach your hand!"
  Binnorie, O Binnorie!
" And ye shall be heir of half my land,"
  By the bonny mill-dams o' Binnorie.

" O sister, I'll not reach my hand,"
  Binnorie, O Binnorie!
" And I'll be heir of all your land,"
  By the bonny mill-dams o' Binnorie.   40

" Shame fa' the hand that I should take,"
  Binnorie, O Binnorie!
" It's twinèd me and my world's make,"
  By the bonny mill-dams o' Binnorie.

" O sister, reach me but your glove!"
  Binnorie, O Binnorie!
" And sweet William shall be your love,"
  By the bonny mill-dams o' Binnorie.

" Sink on, nor hope for hand or glove,"
  Binnorie, O Binnorie!   50
" And sweet William shall better be my love,"
  By the bonny mill-dams o' Binnorie.

"Your cherry cheeks and your yellow hair,"
Binnorie, O Binnorie!
"Garr'd me gang maiden evermair,"
By the bonnie mill-dams o' Binnorie.

Sometimes she sunk, and sometimes she swam,
Binnorie, O Binnorie!
Until she came to the miller's dam,
By the bonny mill-dams o' Binnorie. 60

"O father, father, draw your dam!"
Binnorie, O Binnorie!
"There 's either a mermaid or a milk-white swan,"
By the bonny mill-dams o' Binnorie.

The miller hasted and drew his dam,
Binnorie, O Binnorie!
And there he found a drown'd woman,
By the bonny mill-dams o' Binnorie.

You could not see her yellow hair,
Binnorie, O Binnorie! 70
For gowd and pearls that were sae rare,
By the bonny mill-dams o' Binnorie.

You could na see her middle sma',
Binnorie, O Binnorie!
Her gowden girdle was sae bra',
By the bonny mill-dams o' Binnorie.

An' by there came a harper fine,
Binnorie, O Binnorie!
That harpèd to the king at dine,
By the bonny mill-dams o' Binnorie. 80

When he did look that lady upon,
   Binnorie, O Binnorie!
He sigh'd and made a heavy moan,
   By the bonny mill-dams o' Binnorie.

He's ta'en three locks o' her yallow hair,
   Binnorie, O Binnorie!
And wi' them strung his harp sae fair,
   By the bonny mill-dams o' Binnorie.

The first tune he did play and sing,
   Binnorie, O Binnorie!   90
Was, "Farewell to my father the king,"
   By the bonny mill-dams o' Binnorie.

The nextin tune that he play'd syne,
   Binnorie, O Binnorie!
Was, "Farewell to my mother the queen,"
   By the bonny mill-dams o' Binnorie.

The lasten tune that he play'd then,
   Binnorie, O Binnorie!
Was, "Wae to my sister, fair Ellen!"
   By the bonny mill-dams o' Binnorie.   100

KING ESTMERE

Hearken to me, gentlemen,
  Come and you shall hear;
I'll tell you of two of the boldest brether
  That ever born were.

The tone of them was Adler young,
  The tother was King Estmere;
They were as bold men in their deeds
  As any were, far and near.

As they were drinking ale and wine
  Within King Estmere's hall: 10
"When will ye marry a wife, brother,
  A wife to glad us all?"

Then bespake him King Estmere,
  And answered him hastily:
"I know not that lady in any land
  That's able to marry with me."

"King Adland hath a daughter, brother;
  Men call her bright and sheen;
If I were king here in your stead,
  That lady should be my queen."   20

Says, "Rede me, rede me, dear brother,
  Throughout merry England
Where we might find a messenger
  Betwixt us two to send."

Says, "You shall ride yourself, brother;
    I'll bear you company;
Many through false messengers are deceived,
    And I fear lest so should we."

Thus they renisht them to ride
    Of two good renisht steeds;   30
And when they came to King Adland's hall,
    Of red gold shone their weeds.

And when they came to King Adland's hall,
    Before the goodly gate,
There they found good King Adland
    Rearing himself thereat.

"Now Christ thee save, good King Adland,
    Now Christ you save and see!"
Said, "You be welcome, King Estmere,
    Right heartily to me."   40

"You have a daughter," said Adler young,
    "Men call her bright and sheen;
My brother would marry her to his wife
    Of England to be queen."

"Yesterday was at my dear daughter
    The King his son of Spain,
And then she nicked him of 'nay,'
    And I doubt she'll do you the same."

"The King of Spain is a foul paynim,
    And 'lieveth on Mahound,   50
And pity it were that a fair lady
    Should marry a heathen hound."

"But grant to me," says King Estmere,
  "For my love, I you pray,
That I may see your daughter dear
  Before I go hence away."

"Although it is seven years and more
  Since my daughter was in hall,
She shall come once down for your sake,
  To glad my guestès all."   60

Down then came that maiden fair,
  With ladies laced in pall,
And half a hundred of bold knights
  To bring her from bower to hall,
And as many gentle squires
  To tend upon them all.

The talents of gold, were on her head set,
  Hanged low down to her knee,
And every ring on her small finger
  Shone of the crystal free.   70

Says, "God you save, my dear madam,"
  Says, "God you save and see!"
Said, "You be welcome, King Estmere,
  Right welcome unto me;

"And if you love me as you say,
  So well and heartily,
All that ever you are comen about
  Soon sped now it shall be."

Then bespake her father dear:
  "My daughter, I say nay;   80
Remember well the King of Spain
  What he said yesterday;

"He would pull down my halls and castles
  And reave me of my life.
I cannot blame him if he do,
  If I reave him of his wife."

"Your castles and your towers, father,
  Are strongly built about;
And therefore of the King of Spain
  We need not stand in doubt.   90

"Plight me your troth now, King Estmere,
  By heaven and your right hand,
That you will marry me to your wife
  And make me queen of your land."

Then King Estmere he plight his troth
  By heaven and his right hand,
That he would marry her to his wife
  And make her queen of his land.

And he took leave of that lady fair
  To go to his own country,   100
To fetch him dukes and lords and knights,
  That married they might be.

They had not ridden scant a mile,
  A mile forth of the town,
But in did come the King of Spain
  With kempès many a one;

But in did come the King of Spain
  With many a bold barone,
Tone day to marry King Adland's daughter,
  Tother day to carry her home.   110

She sent one after King Estmere
  In all the speed might be,
That he must either turn and fight,
  Or go home and lose his lady.

One while, then, the page he went,
  Another while he ran;
Till he had o'ertaken King Estmere
  I-wis he never blan.

"Tidings, tidings, King Estmere!"
  "What tidings now, my boy?"   120
"O tidings I can tell to you
  That will you sore annoy:

"You had not ridden scant a mile,
  A mile out of the town,
But in did come the King of Spain
  With kempès many a one;

"But in did come the King of Spain
  With many a bold barone,
Tone day to marry King Adland's daughter,
  Tother day to carry her home.   130

"My lady fair she greets you well
  And evermore well by me;
You must either turn again and fight,
  Or go home and lose your lady."

Says, "Rede me, rede me, dear brother,
  My rede shall rise at thee;
Whether it is better to turn and fight,
  Or go home and lose my lady?"

"Now hearken to me," says Adler young,
  "And your rede must rise at me; 140
I quickly will devise a way
  To set thy lady free.

"My mother was a western woman
  And learned in gramary,
And when I learnèd at the school,
  Something she taught it me.

"There grows an herb within this field,
  And-if it were but known;
His colour, which is white and red,
  It will make black and brown; 150

"His colour, which is brown and black,
  It will make red and white;
That sword is not in all England
  Upon his coat will bite.

"And you shall be a harper, brother,
  Out of the north country,
And I'll be your boy so fain of fight
  And bear your harp by your knee.

"And you shall be the best harper
  That ever took harp in hand, 160
And I will be the best singer
  That ever sung in this land.

"It shall be written in our foreheads
  All and in gramary,
That we two are the boldest men
  That are in all Christenty."

And thus they renisht them to ride
  On two good renisht steeds;
And when they came to King Adland's hall
  Of red gold shone their weeds.   170

And when they came to King Adland's hall,
  Until the fair hall-gate,
There they found a proud porter
  Rearing himself thereat.

Says, "Christ thee save, thou proud porter,"
  Says, "Christ thee save and see!"
"Now you be welcome," said the porter,
  "Of what land soever ye be."

"We ben harpers," said Adler young,
  "Come out of the north country;   180
We ben come hither until this place
  This proud wedding for to see."

Said, "And your colour were red and white,
  As it is black and brown,
I would say King Estmere and his brother
  Were comen until this town."

Then they pulled out a ring of gold,
  Laid it on the porter's arm:
"And ever we will thee, proud porter,
  Thou wilt say us no harm."   190

Sore he looked on King Estmere,
  And sore he handled the ring;
Then opened to them the fair hall-gates;
  He let for no kind of thing.

King Estmere he stabled his steed
  So fair at the hall-board;
The froth that came from his bridle-bit
  Light in King Bremor's beard.

Says, "Stable thy steed, thou proud harper,"
  Says, "Stable him in the stall;   200
It doth not beseem a proud harper
  To stable him in a king's hall."

"My lad he is so lither," he said,
  "He will do nought that 's meet;
And is there any man in this hall
  Were able him to beat?"

"Thou speakest proud words," says the King of
    Spain,
  "Thou harper, here to me;
There is a man within this hall
  Will beat thy lad and thee."   210

"O let that man come down," he said,
  "A sight of him would I see;
And when he hath beaten well my lad,
  Then he shall beat of me."

Down then came the kempery-man
  And looked him in the ear;
For all the gold that was under heaven
  He durst not nigh him near.

"And how now, kemp?" said the King of Spain,
  "And how, what aileth thee?"   220
He says, "It is writ in his forehead,
  All and in gramary,
That for all the gold that is under heaven
  I dare not nigh him nigh."

Then King Estmere pulled forth his harp
  And played a pretty thing;
The lady upstart from the board
  And would have gone from the king.

"Stay thy harp, thou proud harper,
  For God's love I pray thee!   230
For and thou plays as thou begins
  Thou'lt till my bride from me."

He struck upon his harp again
  And played a pretty thing;
The lady lough a loud laughter
  As she sat by the king.

Says, "Sell me thy harp, thou proud harper,
  And thy stringès all,
For as many gold nobles thou shalt have
  As here be rings in the hall."   240

"What would ye do with my harp," he said,
  "If I did sell it ye?"
"To play my wife and me a fit
  When married we had be."

"Now sell me," quoth he, "thy bride so gay,
  As she sits by thy knee,
And as many gold nobles I will give
  As leaves ben on a tree."

"And what would ye do with my bride so gay
  If I did sell her thee?   250
More seemly it is for that lady fair
  To wed with me than thee."

He played again both loud and shrill,
  And Adler he did sing—
"O lady, this is thy own true love;
  No harper, but a king.

"O lady, this is thy own true love,
  As plainly thou mayst see,
And I'll rid thee of that foul paynim
  Who parts thy love and thee."   260

The lady looked, the lady blushed,
  And blushed and looked again,
While Adler he hath drawn his brand
  And hath the Sowdan slain.

Up then rose the kempery-men
  And loud they 'gan to cry:
"Ah, traitors, ye have slain our king,
  And therefore ye shall die."

King Estmere threw the harp aside,
  And swithe he drew his brand,   270
And Estmere, he, and Adler young
  Right stiff in stour did stand.

And aye their swords so sore can bite
  Through help of gramary,
That soon they have slain the kempery-men
  Or forced them forth to flee.

King Estmere took that fair lady
  And married her to his wife,
And brought her home to merry England,
  With her to lead his life.   280

THE HEIR OF LINNE

Of all the lords in fair Scotland
  A song I will begin;
Amongst them all there dwelt a lord,
  Which was the unthrifty lord of Linne.

His father and mother were dead him fro,
  And so was the head of all his kin;
To the cards and dice that he did run
  He did neither cease nor blin.

To drink the wine that was so clear,
  With every man he would make merry;   10
And then bespake him John of the Scales,
  Unto the heir of Linne said he:

Says, "How dost thou, lord of Linne?
  Dost either want gold or fee?
Wilt thou not sell thy lands so broad
  To such a good fellow as me?"

"For all my gold is gone," he said,
  "My land, take it unto thee."
"I draw you to record, my lordës all."
  With that he cast him a God's penny.   20

He told him the gold upon the board,
  It wanted never a bare penny.
"That gold is thine, the land is mine;
  The heir of Linne I will be."

"Here's gold enough," saith the heir of Linne,
  "Both for me and my company."
He drunk the wine that was so clear,
  And with every man he made merry.

Within three quarters of a year
  His gold and fee it waxed thin,   30
His merry men were from him gone,
  And left him himself all alone.

He had never a penny left in his purse,
  Never a penny left but three,
And one was brass, and another was lead,
  And another was white money.

"Now welladay!" said the heir of Linne,
  "Now welladay, and woe is me!
For when I was the lord of Linne,
  I neither wanted gold nor fee.   40

"For I have sold my lands so broad,
  And have not left me one penny;
I must go now and take some rede
  Unto Edinburgh, and beg my bread."

He had not been in Edinburgh
  Not three quarters of a year,
But some did give him, and some said nay,
  And some bid "To the deil gang ye!

"For if we should hang any landless fere,
  The first we would begin with thee."   50
"Now welladay!" said the heir of Linne,
  "Now welladay, and woe is me!

s.   4

"For now I have sold my lands so broad,
    That merry man is irk with me;
But when that I was the lord of Linne,
    Then on my land I lived merrily.

"And now I have sold my land so broad,
    That I have not left me one penny!
God be with my father!" he said,
    "On his land he lived merrily."   60

Still in a study there as he stood,
    He unbethought him of a bill—
He unbethought him of a bill
    Which his father had left with him;

Bade him he should never on it look
    Till he was in extreme need;
"And by my faith," said the heir of Linne,
    "Than now I had never more need."

He took the bill, and looked it on,
    Good comfort that he found there;   70
It told him of a castle wall
    Where there stood three chests in fere.

Two were full of the beaten gold,
    The third was full of white money.
He turned then down his bags of bread,
    And filled them full of gold and fee.

Then he did never cease nor blin,
    Till John of the Scales' house he did win.
When that he came to John of the Scales,
    Up at the speer he lookèd then.   80

There sat three lords upon a row,
  And John o' the Scales sat at the board's head,
And John o' the Scales sat at the board's head,
  Because he was the lord of Linne.

And then bespake the heir of Linne,
  To John o' the Scales' wife thus said he;
Said, "Dame, wilt thou not trust me one shot
  That I may sit down in this company?"

"Now Christ's curse on my head," she said,
  "If I do trust thee one penny!"   90
Then bespake a good fellow,
  Which sat by John o' the Scales his knee;

Said, "Have thou here, thou heir of Linne,
  Forty pence I will lend thee;
Some time a good fellow thou hast been;
  And other forty if need be."

They drunken wine that was so clear,
  And every man they made merry;
And then bespake him John o' the Scales,
  Unto the lord of Linne said he;   100

Said, "How dost thou, heir of Linne,
  Since I did buy thy lands of thee?
I will sell it to thee twenty pound better cheap
  Nor ever I did buy it of thee."

"I draw you to record, lordës all."
  With that he cast him a God's penny;
Then he took to his bags of bread,
  And they were full of the gold so red.

4—2

He told him the gold then over the board,
  It wanted never a broad penny. 110
"That gold is thine, the land is mine,
  And heir of Linne again I will be."

"Now welladay!" said John o' the Scales' wife,
  "Welladay, and woe is me!
Yesterday I was the lady of Linne,
  And now I am but John o' the Scales' wife!"

Says, "Have thou here, thou good fellow,
  Forty pence thou did lend me,
Forty pence thou did lend me,
  And forty pound I will give thee. 120

"I'll make thee keeper of my forest,
  Both of the wild deer and the tame,"

.   .   .   .
  .   .   .   .

But then bespake the heir of Linne,
  These were the words, and thus said he,
"Christ's curse light upon my crown,
  If e'er my land stand in any jeopardy!"

BARBARA ALLAN

It was in and about the Martinmas time,
  When the green leaves were a-falling,
That Sir John Græme, in the West Country,
  Fell in love with Barbara Allan.

He sent his men down through the town,
  To the place where she was dwelling;
"O haste and come to my master dear,
  Gin ye be Barbara Allan."

O hooly, hooly rose she up,
  To the place where he was lying,   10
And when she drew the curtain by,
  "Young man, I think you're dying."

"O it's I am sick, and very, very sick,
  And 't is a' for Barbara Allan."
"O the better for me ye's never be,
  Tho' your heart's blood were a-spilling."

"O dinna ye mind, young man," said she,
  "When ye was in the tavern a drinking,
That ye made the healths gae round and round,
  And slighted Barbara Allan?"   20

He turn'd his face unto the wall,
  And death was with him dealing;
"Adieu, adieu, my dear friends all,
  And be kind to Barbara Allan."

And slowly, slowly raise she up,
  And slowly, slowly left him,
And sighing said she could not stay,
  Since death of life had reft him.

She had not gane a mile but twa,
  When she heard the dead-bell ringing,   30
And every jow that the dead-bell geid,
  It cry'd, "Woe to Barbara Allan!"

"O mother, mother, make my bed,
  O make it saft and narrow!
Since my love died for me to-day,
  I'll die for him to-morrow."

LORD RANDAL

"O where hae ye been, Lord Randal, my son?
O where hae ye been, my handsome young man?"
"I hae been to the wild wood; mother, make my
    bed soon,
For I'm weary wi' hunting, and fain wald lie down."

"Where gat ye your dinner, Lord Randal, my son?
Where gat ye your dinner, my handsome young
    man?"
"I dined wi' my true-love; mother, make my bed
    soon,
For I'm weary wi' hunting, and fain wald lie down."

"What gat ye to your dinner, Lord Randal, my son?
What gat ye to your dinner, my handsome young
　　man?"   10
"I gat eels boil'd in broo; mother, make my bed soon,
For I 'm weary wi' hunting, and fain wald lie down."

"What became of your bloodhounds, Lord Randal,
　　my son?
What became of your bloodhounds, my handsome
　　young man?"
"O they swell'd and they died; mother, make my
　　bed soon,
For I 'm weary wi' hunting, and fain wald lie down."

"O I fear ye are poison'd, Lord Randal, my son!
O I fear ye are poison'd, my handsome young man!"
"O yes, I am poison'd; mother, make my bed soon,
For I 'm sick at the heart, and I fain wald lie
　　down."   20

FAIR ANNIE OF ROUGH ROYAL

"O wha will shoe my fu' fair foot?
　　And wha will glove my hand?
And wha will lace my middle jimp,
　　Wi' the new-made London band?

"And wha will kaim my yellow hair,
　　Wi' the new-made silver kaim?
And wha will father my young son,
　　Till Love Gregor come hame?"

"Your father will shoe your fu' fair foot,
　Your mother will glove your hand;　　10
Your sister will lace your middle jimp
　Wi' the new-made London band.

"Your brother will kaim your yellow hair,
　Wi' the new-made silver kaim;
And the king of heaven will father your bairn,
　Till Love Gregor come hame."

"But I will get a bonny boat,
　And I will sail the sea,
For I maun gang to Love Gregor,
　Since he canno come hame to me."　　20

O she has gotten a bonny boat,
　And sail'd the sa't sea faem;
She lang'd to see her ain true-love,
　Since he could no come hame.

"O row your boat, my mariners,
　And bring me to the land,
For yonder I see my love's castle,
　Close by the sa't sea strand."

She has ta'en her young son in her arms,
　And to the door she's gone,　　30
And lang she's knock'd and sair she ca'd,
　But answer got she none.

"O open the door, Love Gregor," she says,
　"O open, and let me in;
For the wind blaws thro' my yellow hair,
　And the rain draps o'er my chin."

"Awa', awa', ye ill woman,
 You're nae come here for good;
You're but some witch, or wile warlock,
 Or mermaid of the flood."   40

"I am neither a witch nor a wile warlock,
 Nor mermaid of the sea,
I am Fair Annie of Rough Royal;
 O open the door to me."

"Gin ye be Annie of Rough Royal—
 And I trust ye are not she—
Now tell me some of the love-tokens
 That past between you and me."

"O dinna you mind now, Love Gregor,
 When we sat at the wine,   50
How we changed the rings frae our fingers?
 And I can show thee thine.

"O yours was good, and good eneugh,
 But ay the best was mine;
For yours was o' the good red goud,
 But mine o' the di'monds fine.

"But open the door now, Love Gregor,
 O open the door I pray,
For your young son that is in my arms
 Will be dead ere it be day."   60

"Awa', awa', ye ill woman,
 For here ye shanno win in;
Gae drown ye in the raging sea,
 Or hang on the gallows-pin."

When the cock had crawn, and day did dawn,
   And the sun began to peep,
Then up raise him Love Gregor,
   And sair, sair did he weep.

"O I dream'd a dream, my mother dear,
   The thoughts o' it gars me greet,   70
That Fair Annie of Rough Royal
   Lay cauld dead at my feet."

"Gin it be for Annie of Rough Royal
   That ye make a' this din,
She stood a' last night at this door,
   But I trow she wan no in."

"O wae betide ye, ill woman,
   An ill dead may ye die!
That ye wouldno open the door to her,
   Nor yet would waken me."   80

O he has gone down to yon shore-side,
   As fast as he could fare;
He saw Fair Annie in her boat
   But the wind it toss'd her sair.

And "Hey, Annie!" and "How, Annie!
   O Annie, winna ye bide?"
But aye the mair that he cried "Annie,"
   The braider grew the tide.

And "Hey, Annie!" and "How, Annie!
   Dear Annie, speak to me!"   90
But aye the louder he cried "Annie,"
   The louder roar'd the sea.

The wind blew loud, the sea grew rough,
   And dash'd the boat on shore;
Fair Annie floats on the raging sea,
   But her young son raise no more.

Love Gregor tare his yellow hair,
   And made a heavy moan;
Fair Annie's corpse lay at his feet,
   But his bonny young son was gone.   100

O cherry, cherry was her cheek,
   And gowden was her hair,
But clay-cold were her rosy lips,
   Nae spark of life was there.

And first he's kissed her cherry cheek,
   And neist he's kissed her chin;
And saftly press'd her rosy lips,
   But there was nae breath within.

"O wae betide my cruel mother,
   And an ill dead may she die!   110
For she turn'd my true-love frae the door,
   When she came sae far to me."

THE GAY GOSHAWK

"O well 's me o' my gay goshawk,
  That he can speak and flee;
He 'll carry a letter to my love,
  Bring back another to me."

"O how can I your true-love ken,
  Or how can I her know?
When frae her mouth I never heard couth,
  Nor wi' my eyes her saw."

"O well sall ye my true-love ken,
  As soon as you her see;   10
For, of a' the flow'rs in fair Englan',
  The fairest flow'r is she.

"At even at my love's bow'r-door
  There grows a bowing birk,
An' sit ye down and sing thereon
  As she gangs to the kirk.

"An' four-and-twenty ladies fair
  Will wash and go to kirk,
But well sall ye my true-love ken,
  For she wears goud on her skirt.   20

"An' four-and-twenty gay ladies
  Will to the mass repair,
But well sall ye my true-love ken,
  For she wears goud on her hair."

O even at that lady's bow'r-door
  There grows a bowin' birk,
An' he sat down and sang thereon,
  As she gaed to the kirk.

"O eat and drink, my marys a',
  The wine flows you among,   30
Till I gang to my shot-window,
  An' hear yon bonny bird's song.

"Sing on, sing on, my bonny bird,
  The song ye sang yestreen,
For I ken by your sweet singin',
  You're frae my true-love sen'."

O first he sang a merry song,
  An' then he sang a grave,
An' then he peck'd his feathers gray,
  To her the letter gave.   40

"Ha, there's a letter frae your love,
  He says he sent you three;
He canna wait your love langer,
  But for your sake he'll die.

"He bids you write a letter to him;
  He says he's sent you five;
He canno wait your love langer,
  Tho' you're the fairest woman alive."

"Ye bid him bake his bridal bread,
  And brew his bridal ale,   50
An' I'll meet him in fair Scotlan'
  Lang, lang or it be stale."

She's done her to her father dear,
  Fa'n low down on her knee:
"A boon, a boon, my father dear,
  I pray you, grant it me."

"Ask on, ask on, my daughter,
  An' granted it sall be;
Except ae squire in fair Scotlan',
  An' him you sall never see."   60

"The only boon my father dear,
  That I do crave of thee,
Is, gin I die in southin lan's,
  In Scotland to bury me.

"An' the firstin kirk that ye come till,
  Ye gar the bells be rung,
An' the nextin kirk that ye come till,
  Ye gar the mass be sung.

"An' the thirdin kirk that ye come till,
  You deal gold for my sake,   70
An' the fourthin kirk that ye come till,
  You tarry there till night."

She's done her to her bigly bow'r,
  As fast as she could fare,
An' she has ta'en a sleepy draught,
  That she had mix'd wi' care.

She's laid her down upon her bed,
  An' soon she's fa'n asleep,
And soon o'er every tender limb
  Cauld death began to creep.   80

Whan night was flown, an' day was come,
  Nae ane that did her see
But thought she was as surely dead
  As ony lady could be.

Her father an' her brothers dear
  Garred make to her a bier;
The tae half was o' guid red gold,
  The tither o' silver clear.

Her mither an' her sisters fair
  Garred work for her a sark;   90
The tae half was o' cambrick fine,
  The tither o' needle-wark.

The firstin kirk that they came till,
  They garred the bells be rung,
An' the nextin kirk that they came till,
  They garred the mass be sung.

The thirdin kirk that they came till,
  They dealt gold for her sake,
An' the fourthin kirk that they came till,
  Lo, there they met her make!   100

"Lay down, lay down the bigly bier,
  Let me the dead look on."
Wi' cherry cheeks and ruby lips
  She lay an' smil'd on him.

"O ae sheave o' your bread, true-love,
  An' ae glass o' your wine,
For I hae fasted for your sake
  These days is fully nine.

"Gang hame, gang hame, my seven bold brothers,
  Gang hame and sound your horn;   110
An' ye may boast in southin lan's
  Your sister's play'd you scorn."

THOMAS RYMER

True Thomas lay o'er yond grassy bank,
  And he beheld a lady gay,
A lady that was brisk and bold,
  Come riding o'er the ferny brae.

Her skirt was of the grass-green silk,
  Her mantle of the velvet fine,
At ilka tett of her horse's mane
  Hung fifty silver bells and nine.

True Thomas he took off his hat,
  And bowed him low down till his knee: 10
"All hail, thou mighty Queen of Heaven!
  For your peer on earth I never did see."

"O no, O no, True Thomas," she says,
  "That name does not belong to me;
I am but the queen of fair Elfland,
  And I'm come here for to visit thee.

"But ye maun go wi' me now, Thomas,
  True Thomas, ye maun go wi' me,
For ye maun serve me seven years,
  Thro' weal or wae, as may chance to be."   20

She turned about her milk-white steed,
   And took True Thomas up behind,
And aye whene'er her bridle rang,
   The steed flew swifter than the wind.

For forty days and forty nights
   He wade thro' red blude to the knee,
And he saw neither sun nor moon,
   But heard the roaring of the sea.

O they rade on, and further on,
   Until they came to a garden green: 30
"Light down, light down, ye lady free,
   Some of that fruit let me pull to thee."

"O no, O no, True Thomas," she says,
   "That fruit maun not be touched by thee,
For a' the plagues that are in hell
   Light on the fruit of this country.

"But I have a loaf here in my lap,
   Likewise a bottle of claret wine,
And now ere we go farther on,
   We'll rest a while, and ye may dine."   40

When he had eaten and drunk his fill;
   "Lay down your head upon my knee,"
The lady said, "ere we climb yon hill,
   And I will show you fairlies three.

"O see not ye yon narrow road,
   So thick beset wi' thorns and briers?
That is the path of righteousness,
   Tho' after it but few enquires.

S.   5

"And see not ye that braid braid road,
   That lies across yon lily leven?   50
That is the path of wickedness,
   Tho' some call it the road to heaven.

"And see not ye that bonny road,
   Which winds about the ferny brae?
That is the road to fair Elfland,
   Where you and I this night maun gae.

"But, Thomas, ye maun hold your tongue,
   Whatever you may hear or see,
For gin ae word you should chance to speak,
   You will ne'er get back to your ain country." 60

He has gotten a coat of the even cloth,
   And a pair of shoes of velvet green,
And till seven years were past and gone
   True Thomas on earth was never seen.

EDWARD

"Why does your brand sae drap wi' bluid,
         Edward, Edward?
Why does your brand sae drap wi' bluid,
   And why sae sad gang ye, O?"
"O, I hae killed my hauke sae guid,
         Mither, mither:
O, I hae killed my hauke sae guid,
   And I had nae mair but he, O."

"Your haukis bluid was nevir sae reid,
        Edward, Edward.   10
Your haukis bluid was nevir sae reid,
  My deir son I tell thee, O."
"O, I hae killed my reid-roan steid,
        Mither, mither:
O, I hae killed my reid-roan steid,
  That erst was sae fair and frie, O."

"Your steid was auld, and ye hae gat mair,
        Edward, Edward:
Your steid was auld, and ye hae gat mair,
  Sum other dule ye drie, O."   20
"O, I hae killed my fadir deir,
        Mither, mither:
O, I hae killed my fadir deir,
  Alas! and wae is me, O!"

"And whatten penance wul ye drie for that,
        Edward, Edward?
And whatten penance wul ye drie for that,
  My deir son, now tell me, O."
"I'll set my feit in yonder boat,
        Mither, mither: 30
I'll set my feit in yonder boat,
  And I'll fare over the sea, O."

"And what wul ye doe wi' your towers and your ha',
        Edward, Edward?
And what wul ye doe wi' your towers and your ha',
  That were sae fair to see, O?"
"I'll let them stand till they doun fa',
        Mither, mither:
I'll let them stand till they doun fa',
  For here never mair maun I be, O."   40

"And what wul ye leive to your bairns and your wife,
　　　　　Edward, Edward?
And what wul ye leive to your bairns and your wife,
　　　Whan ye gang over the sea, O?"
"The warldis room, let them beg throw life,
　　　　　Mither, mither:
The warldis room, let them beg throw life,
　　　For them never mair wul I see, O."

"And what wul ye leive to your ain mither deir,
　　　　　Edward, Edward?　　　　　　　50
And what wul ye leive to your ain mither deir?
　　　My deir son, now tell me, O."
"The curse of hell frae me sall ye beir,
　　　　　Mither, mither:
The curse of hell frae me sall ye beir,
　　　Sic counseils ye gave to me, O."

THE TWA CORBIES

As I was walking all alane,
I heard twa corbies making a mane,
The tane unto the t'other say,
"Where sall we gang and dine to-day?"

"In behint yon auld fail dyke,
I wot there lies a new-slain knight;
And nae body kens that he lies there,
But his hawk, his hound, and lady fair.

"His hound is to the hunting gane,
His hawk to fetch the wild-fowl hame,   10
His lady's ta'en another mate,
So we may mak' our dinner sweet.

"Ye'll sit on his white hause-bane,
And I'll pike out his bonny blue een:
Wi' ae lock o' his gowden hair
We'll theek our nest when it grows bare.

"Mony a one for him makes mane,
But nane sall ken whare he is gane:
O'er his white banes, when they are bare,
The wind sall blaw for evermair."   20

E BAILIFF'S DAUGHTER OF ISLINGTON

There was a youth, and a well-beloved youth,
  And he was a squire's son;
He loved the bailiff's daughter dear,
  That lived in Islington.

She was coy, and she would not believe
  That he did love her so,
No, nor at any time she would
  Any countenance to him show.

But when his friends did understand
  His fond and foolish mind,   10
They sent him up to fair London,
  An apprentice for to bind.

And when he had been seven long years,
   And his love he had not seen:
"Many a tear have I shed for her sake
   When she little thought of me."

All the maids of Islington
   Went forth to sport and play;
All but the bailiff's daughter dear;
   She secretly stole away.   20

She put off her gown of gray,
   And put on her puggish attire;
She is up to fair London gone,
   Her true-love to require.

As she went along the road,
   The weather being hot and dry,
There was she aware of her true-love,
   At length came riding by.

She stept to him, as red as any rose,
   And took him by the bridle-ring: 30
"I pray you, kind sir, give me one penny,
   To ease my weary limb."

"I prithee, sweetheart, canst thou tell me
   Where that thou wast born?"
"At Islington, kind sir," said she,
   "Where I have had many a scorn."

"I prithee, sweetheart, canst thou tell me
   Whether thou dost know
The bailiff's daughter of Islington?"
   "She's dead, sir, long ago."   40

"Then I will sell my goodly steed,
  My saddle and my bow;
I will into some far country,
  Where no man doth me know."

"O stay, O stay, thou goodly youth!
  She's alive, she is not dead;
Here she standeth by thy side,
  And is ready to be thy bride."

"O farewell grief, and welcome joy,
  Ten thousand times and more!   50
For now I have seen my own true-love,
  That I thought I should have seen no more."

YOUNG BENJIE

Of a' the maids o' fair Scotland,
  The fairest was Marjorie;
And young Benjie was her ae true-love,
  And a dear true-love was he.

And wow! but they were lovers dear,
  And loved fu' constantlie;
But ay the mair when they fell out,
  The sairer was their plea.

And they hae quarrelled on a day,
  Till Marjorie's heart grew wae,   10
And she said she'd chuse another luve,
  And let young Benjie gae.

And he was stout, and proud hearted,
   And thought o't bitterlie,
And he's gaen by the wan moon-light,
   To meet his Marjorie.

"O open, open, my true love!
   O open, and let me in!"
"I dare na open, young Benjie,
   My three brothers are within."   20

"Ye lied, ye lied, my bonny burd,
   Sae loud's I hear ye lie;
As I came by the Lowden banks,
   They bade gude e'en to me.

"But fare ye weel, my ae fause love,
   That I hae loved sae lang!
It sets ye chuse another love,
   And let young Benjie gang."

Then Marjorie turned her round about,
   The tear blinding her ee,   30
"I darena, darena let thee in,
   But I'll come down to thee."

Then saft she smiled, and said to him,
   "O what ill hae I done?"
He took her in his armès twa,
   And threw her o'er the linn.

The stream was strang, the maid was stout,
   And laith laith to be dang,
But, ere she wan the Lowden banks,
   Her fair colour was wan.   40

Then up bespak her eldest brother,
 "O see na ye what I see?"
And out then spak her second brother,
 "It's our sister Marjorie!"

Out then spak her eldest brother,
 "O how shall we her ken?"
And out then spak her youngest brother,
 "There's a honey mark on her chin."

Then they've ta'en up the comely corpse,
 And laid it on the ground:
"O wha has killed our ae sister,
 And how can he be found?

"The night it is her low lykewake,
 The morn her burial day,
And we maun watch at mirk midnight,
 And hear what she will say."

Wi' doors ajar, and candle-light,
 And torches burning clear,
The streikit corpse, till still midnight,
 They waked, but naething hear.

About the middle o' the night,
 The cocks began to craw,
And at the dead hour o' the night,
 The corpse began to thraw.

"O wha has done the wrang, sister,
 Or dared the deadly sin?
Wha was sae stout, and feared nae dout,
 As throw ye o'er the linn?"

"Young Benjie was the first ae man,
  I laid my love upon;   70
He was sae stout and proud-hearted,
  He threw me o'er the linn."

"Sall we young Benjie head, sister,
  Sall we young Benjie hang,
Or sall we pike out his twa gray een,
  And punish him ere he gang?"

"Ye mauna Benjie head, brothers,
  Ye mauna Benjie hang,
But ye maun pike out his twa gray e'en,
  And punish him ere he gang.   80

"Tie a green gravat round his neck,
  And lead him out and in,
And the best ae servant about your house,
  To wait young Benjie on.

"And ay, at every seven year's end,
  Ye'll tak him to the linn;
For that's the penance he maun drie,
  To scug his deadly sin."

THE LYKE-WAKE DIRGE

This ae night, this ae night,
  Every night and all,
Fire and fleet and candle-light,
  And Christ receive thy saule!

When thou from hence away art past,
  Every night and all
To Whinny-muir thou comest at last;
  And Christ receive thy saule!

If ever thou gavest hosen and shoon,
  Every night and all   10
Sit thee down and put them on;
  And Christ receive thy saule!

But if hosen and shoon thou never gave none
  Every night and all
The Whins shall prick thee to the bare bone;
  And Christ receive thy saule!

From Whinny-muir when thou mayst pass
  Every night and all
To Brig o' Dread thou comest at last;
  And Christ receive thy saule!   20

From Brig o' Dread when thou mayst pass
  Every night and all
To Purgatory fire thou comest at last;
  And Christ receive thy saule!

If ever thou gavest milk or drink,
   Every night and all
The fire shall never make thee shrink;
   And Christ receive thy saule!

But if milk nor drink thou never gave none,
   Every night and all   30
The fire shall burn thee to the bare bone;
   And Christ receive thy saule!

This ae night, this ae night,
   Every night and all,
Fire and fleet and candle-light,
   And Christ receive thy saule!

THE DEMON LOVER

"O whare hae ye been, my dearest dear,
   These seven lang years and more?"
"O I am come to seek my former vows,
   That ye promised me before."

"Awa' wi' your former vows," she says,
   "Or else ye will breed strife;
Awa' wi' your former vows," she says,
   "For I'm become a wife.

"I am married to a ship-carpenter,
   A ship-carpenter he's bound;   10
I wadna he ken'd my mind this nicht
   For twice five hundred pound."
   *   *   *   *   *   *   *

She has put her foot on gude ship-board,
  And on ship-board she's gane,
And the veil that hung o'er her face
  Was a' wi' gowd begane.

She had na sailed a league, a league,
  A league but barely twa,
Till she did mind on the husband she left,
  And her wee young son alsua.   20

"O haud your tongue, my dearest dear,
  Let all your follies a-be;
I'll show whare the white lillies grow,
  On the banks of Italie."

She had na sailed a league, a league,
  A league but barely three,
Till grim, grim grew his countenance,
  And gurly grew the sea.

"O haud your tongue, my dearest dear,
  Let all your follies a-be;   30
I'll show whare the white lillies grow,
  In the bottom of the sea."

He's ta'en her by the milk-white hand,
  And he's thrown her in the main;
And full five-and-twenty hundred ships
  Perish'd all on the coast of Spain.

FAIR HELEN OF KIRCONNELL

I wish I were where Helen lies,
Night and day on me she cries,
O that I were where Helen lies,
  On fair Kirconnell Lee!

Curst be the heart that thought the thought,
And curst the hand that fired the shot,
When in my arms burd Helen dropt,
  And died to succour me.

O think na ye my heart was sair,
When my love dropt down and spak nae mair? 10
There did she swoon wi' meikle care,
  On fair Kirconnell Lee.

As I went down the water side,
None but my foe to be my guide,
None but my foe to be my guide,
  On fair Kirconnell Lee.

I lighted down, my sword did draw,
I hackèd him in pieces sma',
I hackèd him in pieces sma',
  For her sake that died for me.   20

O Helen fair, beyond compare,
I'll make a garland of thy hair,
Shall bind my heart for evermair,
  Untill the day I die.

O that I were where Helen lies,
Night and day on me she cries,
Out of my bed she bids me rise,
  Says, "Haste, and come to me!"

O Helen fair! O Helen chaste!
If I were with thee I were blest,   30
Where thou lies low, and takes thy rest,
  On fair Kirconnell Lee.

I wish my grave were growing green,
A winding-sheet drawn ower my e'en
And I in Helen's arms lying
  On fair Kirconnell Lee.

I wish I were where Helen lies,
Night and day on me she cries,
And I am weary of the skies,
  For her sake that died for me.   40

THE BONNY EARL OF MURRAY

Ye Highlands and ye Lawlands,
  Oh! where have you been?
They have slain the Earl of Murray,
  And they lay'd him on the green!

Now wae be to thee, Huntly,
  And wherefore did you sae?
I bade you bring him wi' you,
  But forbade you him to slay.

He was a braw gallant,
  And he rid at the ring;   10
And the bonny Earl of Murray,
  Oh! he might have been a King.

He was a braw gallant,
  And he play'd at the ba';
And the bonny Earl of Murray
  Was the flower amang them a'.

He was a braw gallant,
  And he play'd at the glove;
And the bonny Earl of Murray,
  Oh! he was the Queen's love.   20

Oh! lang will his lady
  Look o'er the castle Down,
E'er she see the Earl of Murray
  Come sounding thro' the town.

BONNIE GEORGE CAMPBELL

  Hie upon Hielands
    And low upon Tay,
  Bonnie George Campbell
    Rade out on a day.
  Saddled and bridled
    And gallant rade he;
  Hame came his gude horse,
    But never cam he!

Out cam his auld mither
  Greeting fu' sair,   10
And out cam his bonnie bride
  Rivin' her hair.
Saddled and bridled
  And booted rade he;
Toom hame cam the saddle,
  But never cam he!

"My meadow lies green,
  And my corn is unshorn;
My barn is to big,
  And my babie's unborn."   20
Saddled and bridled
  And booted rade he;
Toom hame cam the saddle,
  But never cam he!

THE TWA BROTHERS

There were twa brethren in the north,
  They went to the school thegithar;
The one unto the other said,
  "Will you try a warsle afore?"

They warsled up, they warsled down,
  Till Sir John fell to the ground,
And there was a knife in Sir Willie's pouch,
  Gied him a deadlie wound.

"O brither dear, take me on your back,
  Carry me to yon burn clear,   10
And wash the blood from off my wound,
  And it will bleed nae mair."

He took him up upon his back,
  Carried him to yon burn clear,
And washed the blood from off his wound,
  But aye it bled the mair.

"Oh brither dear, take me on your back,
  Carry me to yon kirk-yard,
And dig a grave baith wide and deep,
  And lay my body there."   20

He's ta'en him up upon his back,
  Carried him to yon kirk-yard,
And dug a grave baith deep and wide,
  And laid his body there.

"But what will I say to my father dear,
  Gin he chance to say, Willie, whar's John?"
"Oh say that he's to England gone,
  To buy him a cask of wine."

"And what will I say to my mother dear,
  Gin she chance to say, Willie, whar's John?" 30
"Oh say that he's to England gone,
  To buy her a new silk gown."

"And what will I say to my sister dear,
  Gin she chance to say, Willie, whar's John?"
"Oh say that he's to England gone,
  To buy her a wedding ring."

"But what will I say to her you lo'e dear,
  Gin she cry, Why tarries my John?"
"Oh tell her I lie in Kirk-land fair,
  And home again never will come."   40

FAIR ANNIE

"O I'm ga'en o'er the sea, Fair Annie,
   A braw bride to bring hame.
Wi' her I will get gowd and gear;
   Wi' you I ne'er got nane.

"But wha will bake my bridal bread,
   Or brew my bridal ale?
And wha will welcome my brisk bride,
   That I bring o'er the dale?"

"It's I will bake your bridal bread,
   And brew your bridal ale;   10
And I will welcome your brisk bride,
   That you bring o'er the dale."

"But she that welcomes my brisk bride
   Maun gang like maiden fair;
She maun lace on her robe sae jimp,
   And braid her yellow hair."

She's ta'en her young son in her arms,
   Another in her hand,
And she's up to the highest tower,
   To see him come to land.   20

"Come up, come up, my eldest son,
   And look o'er yon sea-strand,
And see your father's new-come bride,
   Before she come to land."

"Come down, come down, my mother dear,
  Come frae the castle wa'!
I fear, if langer ye stand there,
  Ye'll let yoursel' down fa'."

And she gaed down, and farther down,
  Her love's ship for to see,   30
And the topmast and the mainmast
  Shone like the silver free.

And she's gaen down, and farther down,
  The bride's ship to behold,
And the topmast and the mainmast
  They shone just like the gold.

She's ta'en her seven sons in her hand,
  I wot she didna fail;
She met Lord Thomas and his bride,
  As they came o'er the dale.   40

"You're welcome to your house, Lord Thomas,
  You're welcome to your land;
You're welcome with your fair lady,
  That you lead by the hand.

"You're welcome to your ha's, lady,
  You're welcome to your bowers;
You're welcome to your hame, lady,
  For a' that's here is yours."

"I thank thee, Annie, I thank thee, Annie,
  Sae dearly as I thank thee;   50
You're the likest to my sister Annie,
  That ever I did see.

"There came a knight out o'er the sea,
  And steal'd my sister away;
The shame scoup in his company,
  And land where'er he gae!"

She hang ae napkin at the door,
  Another in the ha',
And a' to wipe the trickling tears,
  Sae fast as they did fa'.   60

And aye she served the long tables
  With white bread and with wine;
And aye she drank the wan water
  To haud her colour fine.

And aye she served the lang tables,
  With white bread and with brown;
And aye she turned her round about,
  Sae fast the tears fell down.

And he's ta'en down the silk napkin,
  Hung on a silver pin,   70
And aye he wipes the tear trickling
  A' down her cheek and chin.

And aye he turned him round about,
  And smiled amang his men;
Says, "Like ye best the old lady,
  Or her that's new come hame?"

When bells were rung, and mass was sung,
  And a' men bound to bed,
Lord Thomas and his new-come bride
  To their chamber they were gaed.   80

Annie made her bed a little forbye,
　To hear what they might say;
"And ever alas," Fair Annie cried,
　"That I should see this day!

"Gin my seven sons were seven young rats,
　Running on the castle wa',
And I were a gray cat mysel',
　I soon would worry them a'.

"Gin my seven sons were seven young hares,
　Running o'er yon lily lee,   90
And I were a grew-hound mysel',
　Soon worried they a' should be."

And wae and sad Fair Annie sat,
　And dreary was her sang,
And ever, as she sobb'd and grat,
　"Wae to the man that did the wrang!"

"My gown is on," said the new-come bride,
　"My shoes are on my feet,
And I will to Fair Annie's chamber,
　And see what gars her greet.   100

"What ails ye, what ails ye, Fair Annie,
　That ye make sic a moan?
Has your wine barrels cast the girds,
　Or is your white bread gone?

"O wha was't was your father, Annie,
　Or wha was't was your mother?
And had ye ony sister, Annie,
　Or had ye ony brother?"

"The Earl of Wemyss was my father,
  The Countess of Wemyss my mother;   110
And a' the folk about the house
  To me were sister and brother."

"If the Earl of Wemyss was your father,
  I wot sae he was mine;
And it shall not be for lack o' gowd
  That ye your love sall tyne.

"I 've seven ships upon the sea
  All loaded to the brim,
And five of them I 'll give to thee,
  And twa shall carry me hame."   120

THE CRUEL BROTHER

There was three ladies play'd at the ba',
  With a hey ho and a lillie gay
There came a knight and played o'er them a',
  As the primrose spreads so sweetly.

The eldest was baith tall and fair,
But the youngest was beyond compare.

The midmost had a graceful mien,
But the youngest look'd like beauty's queen.

The knight bow'd low to a' the three,
But to the youngest he bent his knee.

The lady turned her head aside;
The knight he woo'd her to be his bride.   10

The lady blush'd a rosy red,
And say'd, "Sir knight, I 'm too young to wed."

"O lady fair, give me your hand,
And I 'll make you lady of a' my land."

"Sir knight, ere ye my favour win,
You maun get consent frae a' my kin."

He 's got consent frae her parents dear,
And likewise frae her sisters fair.

He 's got consent frae her kin each one,
But forgot to speak to her brother John.   20

Now, when the wedding day was come,
The knight would take his bonny bride home.

And many a lord and many a knight
Came to behold that lady bright.

And there was nae man that did her see,
But wish'd himself bridegroom to be.

Her father dear led her down the stair,
And her sisters twain they kiss'd her there.

Her mother dear led her thro' the close,
And her brother John set her on her horse.   30

She lean'd her o'er the saddle-bow,
To give him a kiss ere she did go.

He has ta'en a knife, baith lang and sharp,
And stabb'd that bonny bride to the heart.

She hadno ridden half thro' the town,
Until her heart's blude stain'd her gown.

"Ride softly on," says the best young man,
"For I think our bonny bride looks pale and wan."

"O lead me gently up yon hill,
And I'll there sit down, and make my will."   40

"O what will you leave to your father dear?"
"The silver-shod steed that brought me here."

"What will you leave to your mother dear?"
"My velvet pall and my silken gear."

"What will you leave to your sister Anne?"
"My silken scarf and my gowden fan."

"What will you leave to your sister Grace?"
"My bloody clothes to wash and dress."

"What will you leave to your brother John?"
"The gallows-tree to hang him on."   50

"What will you leave to your brother John's wife?"
"The wilderness to end her life."

This lady fair in her grave was laid,
And many a mass was o'er her said.

But it would have made your heart right sair,
To see the bridegroom rive his hair.

YOUNG WATERS

About Yule, when the wind blew cule,
    And the round tables began,
A, there is cum to our king's court
    Mony a well-favour'd man.

The queen luikt owre the castle-wa',
    Beheld baith dale and down,
And there she saw Young Waters
    Cum riding to the town.

His footmen they did rin before,
    His horsemen rade behind;   10
Ane mantel of the burning gowd
    Did keip him frae the wind.

Gowden-graith'd his horse before,
    And siller-shod behind;
The horse Young Waters rade upon
    Was fleeter than the wind.

Out then spake a wylie lord,
    Unto the queen said he:
"O tell me wha's the fairest face
    Rides in the company?"   20

"I've seen lord, and I've seen laird,
    And knights of high degree,
But a fairer face than Young Waters
    Mine eyne did never see."

Out then spake the jealous king,
  And an angry man was he:
"O if he had bin twice as fair,
  You micht have excepted me."

"You're neither laird nor lord," she says,
  "But the king that wears the crown; 30
There is not a knight in fair Scotland
  But to thee maun bow down."

For a' that she could do or say,
  Appeased he wad nae be,
But for the words which she had said,
  Young Waters he maun die.

They hae ta'en Young Waters,
  And put fetters to his feet;
They hae ta'en Young Waters,
  And thrown him in dungeon deep. 40

"Aft have I ridden thro' Stirling town,
  In the wind but and the weit;
But I ne'er rade thro' Stirling town
  Wi' fetters at my feet.

"Aft have I ridden thro' Stirling town,
  In the wind but and the rain;
But I ne'er rade thro' Stirling town
  Ne'er to return again."

They hae ta'en to the heading-hill
  His young son in his cradle, 50
And they hae ta'en to the heading-hill
  His horse but and his saddle.

They hae ta'en to heading-hill
  His lady fair to see,
And for the words the queen had spoke
  Young Waters he did die.

BROWN ADAM

O wha would wish the win' to blaw,
  Or the green leaves fa' therewith?
Or wha wad wish a leeler love
  Than Brown Adam the Smith?

His hammer's o' the beaten gold,
  His study's o' the steel,
His fingers white are my delite,
  He blows his bellows well.

But they ha' banish'd him, Brown Adam,
  Frae father and frae mither,   10
An' they ha' banish'd him, Brown Adam,
  Frae sister and frae brither.

And they ha' banish'd Brown Adam
  Frae the flow'r o' a' his kin;
An' he's biggit a bow'r i' the good green wood
  Between his lady an' him.

O it fell once upon a day
  Brown Adam he thought lang,
An' he would to the green wood gang,
  To hunt some venison.   20

He's ta'en his bow his arm o'er,
　His bran' intill his han',
And he is to the good green wood,
　As fast as he could gang.

O he's shot up, an' he's shot down,
　The bird upo' the briar,
An' he's sent it hame to his lady,
　Bade her be of good cheer.

O he's shot up, an' he's shot down,
　The bird upo' the thorn,   30
And sent it hame to his lady,
　And he'd he hame the morn.

When he came till his lady's bow'r-door
　He stood a little forbye,
And there he heard a fu' fa'se knight
　Temptin' his gay lady.

O he's ta'en out a gay gold ring,
　Had cost him mony a poun':
"O grant me love for love, lady,
　An' this sall be your own."   40

"I loo Brown Adam well," she says,
　"I wot sae does he me;
An' I would na gi' Brown Adam's love
　For nae fa'se knight I see."

Out he has ta'en a purse of gold,
　Was a' fu' to the string:
"Grant me but love for love, lady,
　An' a' this sall be thine."

"I loo Brown Adam well," she says,
  "An' I ken sae does he me: 50
An' I wouldna be your light leman
  For mair nor ye could gie."

Then out has he drawn his lang, lang bran',
  An' he's flash'd it in her een:
"Now grant me love for love, lady,
  Or thro' you this sall gang!"

"O," sighing said that gay lady,
  "Brown Adam tarries lang!"
Then up it starts Brown Adam,
  Says, "I'm just at your han'."   60

He's gard him leave his bow, his bow,
  He's gard him leave his bran';
He's gard him leave a better pledge—
  Four fingers o' his right han'.

KING EDWARD AND THE TANNER
OF TAMWORTH

In summer time, when leaves grow green,
  And blossoms bedeck the tree,
King Edward would a hunting ride,
  Some pastime for to see.

With hawk and hound he made him bowne,
  With horn, and eke with bow;
To Drayton Basset he took his way,
  With all his lords a-row.

And he had ridden o'er dale and down
  By eight of clock in the day,   10
When he was ware of a bold tanner,
  Come riding along the way.

A fair russet coat the tanner had on
  Fast buttoned under his chin,
And under him a good cow-hide,
  And a mare of four shilling.

"Now stand you still, my good lords all,
  Under the green wood spray;
And I will wend to yonder fellow,
  To weet what he will say."—   20

"God speed, God speed thee," said our king.
  "Thou art welcome, Sir," said he.
"The readiest way to Drayton Basset
  I pray thee to shew to me."

"To Drayton Basset wouldst thou go,
  Fro the place where thou dost stand?
The next pair of gallows thou comest unto,
  Turn in upon thy right hand."

"That is an unready way," said our king,
  "Thou dost but jest, I see;   30
Now shew me out the nearest way,
  And I pray thee wend with me."

"Away with a vengeance!" quoth the tanner:
  "I hold thee out of thy wit:
All day have I ridden on Brock my mare,
  And I am fasting yet."

"Go with me down to Drayton Basset,
  No dainties we will spare;
All day shalt thou eat and drink of the best,
  And I will pay thy fare."   40

"Gramercy for nothing," the tanner replied,
  ."Thou payest no fare of mine:
I trow I've more nobles in my purse,
  Than thou hast pence in thine."

"God give thee joy of them," said the king,
  "And send them well to prief."
The tanner would fain have been away,
  For he weened he had been a thief.

"What art thou," he said, "thou fine fellow?
  Of thee I am in great fear,   50
For the clothes thou wearest upon thy back
  Might beseem a lord to wear."

"I never stole them," quoth our king,
  "I tell you, Sir, by the rood."
"Then thou playest, as many an unthrift doth,
  And standest in midds of thy good."

"What tidings hear you," said the king,
  "As you ride far and near?"
"I hear no tidings, Sir, by the mass,
  But that cow-hides are dear."   60

"Cow-hides! cow-hides! what things are those?
  I marvel what they be?"
"What, art thou a fool?" the tanner replied;
  "I carry one under me."

"What craftsman art thou?" said the king,
  "I pray thee tell me trow."
"I am a barker, Sir, by my trade;
  Now tell me what art thou?"

"I am a poor courtier, Sir," quoth he,
  "That am forth of service worn;   70
And fain I would thy prentice be,
  Thy cunning for to learn."

"Marry, heaven forfend," the tanner replied,
  "That thou my prentice were:
Thou wouldst spend more good than I should win
  By forty shilling a year."

"Yet one thing would I," said our king,
  "If thou wilt not seem strange:
Though my horse be better than thy mare,
  Yet with thee I fain would change."   80

"Why, if with me thou fain wilt change,
  As change full well may we,
By the faith of my body, thou proud fellow,
  I will have some boot of thee."

"That were against reason," said the king,
  "I swear, so mote I thee,
My horse is better than thy mare,
  And that thou well mayst see."

"Yea, Sir, but Brock is gentle and mild,
  And softly she will fare: 90
Thy horse is unruly and wild, I wis;
  Aye skipping here and there."

S.   7

"What boot wilt thou have?" our king replied;
  "Now tell me in this stound."
"No pence nor half pence, by my fay,
  But a noble in gold so round."

"Here's twenty groats of white money,
  Sith thou will have it of me."
"I would have sworn, now," quoth the tanner,
  "Thou hadst not had one penny.   100

"But since we two have made a change,
  A change we must abide,
Although thou hast gotten Brock my mare,
  Thou gettest not my cow-hide."

"I will not have it," said the king,
  "I swear, so mote I thee;
Thy foul cow-hide I would not bear,
  If thou wouldst give it to me."

The tanner he took his good cow-hide,
  That of the cow was hilt;   110
And threw it upon the king's sadell,
  That was so fairly gilt.

"Now help me up, thou fine fellow,
  'Tis time that I were gone:
When I come home to Gillian my wife,
  She'll say I am a gentleman."

When the tanner he was in the king's sadell,
  And his foot in the stirrup was;
He marvelled greatly in his mind,
  Whether it were gold or brass.   120

But when his steed saw the cow's tail wag,
  And eke the black cow-horn,
He stamped, and stared, and away he ran,
  As the devil had him borne.

The tanner he pull'd, the tanner he sweat,
  And held by the pummel fast:
At length the tanner came tumbling down;
  His neck he had well-nigh brast.

"Take thy horse again, with a vengeance," he said,
  "With me he shall not bide."   130
"My horse would have borne thee well enough,
  But he knew not of thy cow-hide.

"Yet if again thou fain wouldst change,
  As change full well may we,
By the faith of my body, thou jolly tanner,
  I will have some boot of thee."

"What boot wilt thou have?" the tanner replied,
  "Now tell me in this stounde."
"No pence nor halfpence, Sir, by my fay,
  But I will have twenty pound."   140

"Here's twenty groats out of my purse;
  And twenty I have of thine:
And I have one more, which we will spend
  Together at the wine."

The king set a bugle horn to his mouth,
  And blew both loud and shrill:
And soon came lords, and soon came knights,
  Fast riding over the hill.

"Now, out alas!" the tanner he cried,
  "That ever I saw this day!   150
Thou art a strong thief; yon come thy fellows
  Will bear my cow-hide away."

"They are no thieves," the king replied,
  "I swear, so mote I thee:
But they are the lords of the north country,
  Here come to hunt with me."

And soon before our king they came,
  And knelt down on the ground:
Then might the tanner have been away,
  He had lever than twenty pound.   160

"A collar, a collar, here!" said the king,
  "A collar," he loud gan cry:
Then would he lever than twenty pound,
  He had not been so nigh.

"A collar, a collar," the tanner he said,
  "I trow it will breed sorrow:
After a collar cometh a halter,
  And I shall be hanged to-morrow."

"Away with thy fear, thou jolly tanner,
  For the sport thou hast shown to me,   170
I wot no halter thou shalt wear,
  But thou shalt have a knight's fee.

"For Plumpton Park I will give thee
  With tenements fair beside;
'Tis worth three hundred marks by the year,
  To maintain thy good cow-hide."

"Gramercy, my liege," the tanner replied,
  "For the favour thou hast me shown;
If ever thou comest to merry Tamworth,
  Neat's-leather shall clout thy shoon."   180

WILL STEWART AND JOHN

It's by two men I sing my song;
  Their name is William Stewart and John.
William he is the elder brother,
  But John he is the wiser man.

But William is in care-bed laid,
  And for the love of a fair lady;
If he have not the love of the Earl of Mar's daughter,
  In faith, for love that he must die.

Then John was sorry for his brother,
  To see him lie and languish so: 10
"What do you mourn for, brother?" he says,
  "I pray you tell to me your woe.

"Do you mourn for gold, brother?
  Or do you mourn for fee?
Or do you mourn for a likesome lady,
  You never saw her with your ee?"

"I do not mourn for gold," he says,
  "Nor I do not mourn for any fee;
But I do mourn for a likesome lady,
  I ne'er blinked on her with mine ee."   20

"But when harvest is gotten, my dear brother—
   All this is true that I tell thee—
Gentlemen they love hunting well,
   And give wight-men their cloth and fee.

"Then I'll go a wooing for thy sake,
   In all the speed that I can gone,
And for to see this likesome lady,
   And hope to send thee good tidings home."

John Stewart is gone a-wooing for his brother
   So far into fair Scotland;   30
And left his brother in mickle fear
   Until he hear the good tydand.

And when he came to the Earl of Mar's house,
   So well he could his courtesy;
And when he came before the Earl,
   He kneeled low down upon his knee.

"O rise up, rise up, John Stewart!
   Rise up now, I do bid thee;
How doth thy father, John Stewart,
   And all the lords in his country?"   40

"And it please you, my lord, my father's dead;
   My brother and I cannot agree;
My brother and I am fallen at discord,
   And I am come to crave a service of thee."

"O welcome, welcome, John Stewart,
   A welcome man thou art to me;
I'll make thee chamberlain to my daughter,
   And for to tend of that lady so free.

"And if thou wilt have a better office,
　Ask, and thou shalt have it of me;　　　50
And where I give others a penny of wage,
　In faith, John, thou shalt have three."

And then bespake him John Stewart,
　And these were the words said he:
"There is no office in your court
　This day that better pleaseth me."

The Friday is gone, the Sunday is come;
　All this is true that I do say;
And to the church that they be gone,
　John Stewart and the lady gay.　　　60

And as they did come home again
　(I-wis it was a meeten mile),
John Stewart and the lady gay,
　They thought it but a little while.

"I am a messenger, lady," he says,
　"I am a messenger to thee."
"O speak for thyself, John Stewart," she says,
　"A welcome man that thou shalt be."

"Nay, by my faith," says John Stewart,
　"Which, ever alas! that may not be;　　　70
He hath a higher degree in honour,
　Alas, lady, than ever I.

"He is a lord, now, born by birth,
　And an earl after his father doth die;
His hair is yellow, his eyes ben gray;
　All this is true that I tell ye.

"He is fine in the middle, and small in the waist,
   And pleasant in a woman's eye;
And more nor this—he dies for your love;
   Therefore, lady, show some pity."   80

"If this be so," then says the lady,
   "If this be true that thou tells me,
By my faith, then, John Stewart,
   I can love him heartily.

"Bid him meet me at St Patrick's Church,
   On Sunday after St Andrew's day;
The flower of Scotland will be there,
   And then begins our summer's play.

"And bid him bring with him a hundred gunners,
   And rank riders let them be,—   90
And let them be of the rankest riders
   That be to be found in that country.

"The best and worst, and all in like,
   Bid him clothe them in one livery;
And for his men green is the best,
   And green now let their liveries be.

"And clothe himself in scarlet red,
   That is so seemly for to see;
For scarlet is a fair colour
   And pleasant in a woman's ee.   100

"He must play sixteen games at ball,
   Against the men of this country;
And if he win the greater part,
   Then I shall love him more tenderly."

What the lady said, John Stewart writ,
  And to Argyle Castle sent it he;
And when Willie Stewart saw the letter,
  Forth of care-bed then lope he.

He mustered together his merry men all,
  He mustered them so lovelily;   110
He thought he had scarce on half a hundred,
  Then had he eleven score and three.

He chose forth a hundred of the best
  That were to be found in that country;
He clad them all in one colour,
  And green i-wis their liveries be.

He clad himself in scarlet red,
  That is so seemly for to see;
For scarlet is a fair colour
  And seemly in a woman's ee.   120

And then towards Patrick's Church he went,
  With all his men in brave array,
To get a sight, if that he might,
  And speak with his lady gay.

When they came to Patrick's Church,
  She kneeled down by her mother truly:
"O mother, if it please you to give me leave,
  The Stewart's horse fain would I see."

"I'll give you leave, my dear daughter,
  And I and my maid will go with ye."   130
The lady had rather have gone herself,
  Than have had her mother's company.

When they came before Willie Stewart,
  So well he could his courtesy.
"I would kiss your daughter, lady," he said,
  "And-if your will that so it be."

The lady's mother was content
  To do a stranger that courtesy;
And when Willie had gotten a kiss,
  I-wis she might have teemed him three.   140

Sixteen games were played that day there;
  This is the truth that I do say;
Willie Stewart and his merry men,
  They carried twelve of them away.

And when the games that they were done,
  And all the folks away were gone
But the Earl of Mar and William Stewart,
  The Earl would needs have William home.

And when they came unto the Earl's house,
  They walkèd to a garden green;   150
For to confer of their business
  Into the garden they be gone.

"I love your daughter," says William Stewart,
  "But I cannot tell whether she loveth me."
"Marry, God defend," says the Earl of Mar,
  "That ever so that it should be!

"I had rather a gallows there was made,
  And hang thee for my daughter's sake;
I had rather a fire were made at a stake,
  And burn thee for my daughter's sake!   160

"To chamber, to chamber, gay lady," he says,
  "In the devil's name now I bid thee!
And thou get thee not to thy chamber soon,
  I'll beat thee before the Stewart's eye."

And then bespake William Stewart,
  These were the words that then said he:
"If thou beat thy daughter for my sake,
  Thou'st beat a hundred men and me."

Then bespake John Stewart;
  Lord, an angry man was he!   170
"O churl, if thou wouldst not have matched with my
      brother,
  Thou might have answered him courteously."

"O hold thy peace, John Stewart,
  And chamber thy words now, I bid thee;
If thou chamber not thy words soon,
  Thou'st lose a good service—so shalt thou do me."

"Marry, hang them that cares," says John Stewart,
  "Either for thy service or for thee;
Services can I have enough;
  But brethren we must ever be."   180

William Stewart and his brother John
  To Argyle Castle gone they be;
And when Willie came to Argyle Castle,
  Into care-bed then lope he.

A Parliament at Edinburgh was made,
  The King and his nobles all met there;
They sent for William Stewart and John,
  To come amongst the other peers.

Their clothing was of scarlet red,
 That was so seemly for to see;   190
Black hats, white feathers plewed with gold,
 And set all on their heads truly.

Their stockings were of twisted silk,
 With garters fringed about with gold;
Their shoes were of the cordevain,
 And all was comely to behold.

And when they came to Edinburgh,
 They called for John Stewart and Willie.
"I answer in a lord's room," says Will Stewart,
 "But an earl I hope to be."   200

"Come down, come down," says the Lord of Mar,
 "I knew not what was thy degree."
"O churl, if I might not have matched with thy
  daughter,
 It had not been 'long of my degree.

"My father he is the King his brother,
 The King is uncle unto me;
O churl, if I might not have matched with thy
  daughter,
 It had not been 'long of my degree."

"O hold your peace," then said the King,
 "Cousin William, I do bid thee;   210
In faith, cousin William, he loves you the worse
 Because you are akin to me.

"I'll make thee an earl with a silver wand,
 And add more honours still to thee;
Thy brother John shall be a lord
 Of the best at home in his country.

"Thy brother Kester shall be a knight;
  Lands and livings I will him give,
And still he shall live in court with me,
  And I'll maintain him whilst he doth live."   220

And when the Parliament was done
  And all the folks away were gone,
Willie Stewart and John his brother,
  To Argyle Castle they be gone.

But when they came to Argyle Castle,
  That was so far in that country,
He thought so much then of his love
  That into care-bed then lope he.

John Stewart did see his brother so ill,
  Lord, in his heart that he was woe!   230
"I will go wooing for thy sake
  Again yonder gay lady to.

"I'll clothe myself in strange array;
  In a beggar's habit I will go,
That when I come before the Earl of Mar
  My clothing strange he shall not know."

John he got on a clouted cloak,
  So meet and low then by his knee,
With four garters upon one leg,
  Two above and two below truly.   240

"But if thou be a beggar, brother,
  Thou art a beggar that is unknown;
For thou art one of the stoutest beggars
  That ever I saw since I was born.

"Here, give the lady this gay gold ring,
  A token to her that is well known;
And if she but advise it well,
  She'll know sometime it was her own."

"Stay, by my faith, I go not yet,"
  John Stewart he can reply;   250
"I'll have my bottle full of beer,
  The best that is in thy buttery.

"I'll have my satchel filled full of meat;
  I am sure it will do no harm;
For before I come to the Earl of Mar's house,
  My lips, I am sure, they will be warm."

And when he came to the Earl of Mar's house,
  By chance it was of the dole-day;
But John could find no place to stand,
  Until he came to the lady gay.   260

But many a beggar he threw down,
  And made them all with weeping say:
"He is the devil; he is no beggar;
  That is come forth of some strange country."

And now the dole that it is dealt,
  And all the beggars be gone away,
Saving John Stewart, that seemed a beggar,
  And the lady that was so gay.

"Lady," says John, "I am no beggar,
  As by my clothes you may think that I be;   270
I am your servant, John Stewart,
  And sent a messenger to thee."

"But if thou be John Stewart,
 As I do think that so thou be,
Avale thy cap, avale thy hood,
 And I will stand and speak to thee.

"How doth thy brother, John Stewart,
 And all the lords in his country?"
"O fie upon thee, wicked woman!
 My brother he doth the worse for thee."   280

With that, the tears stood in her eyes;
 O Lord, she wept so tenderly!
Says, "Lay the blame unto my father;
 I pray you lay it not to me.

"Commend me to my own true-love,
 That lives so far in the North country,
And bid him meet me at Martingsdale
 Fully within these dayès three.

"Hang them," says the lady gay,
 "That lets their father witting be!   290
I'll prove a lady full of love,
 And be there by the sun be a quarter high.

"And bid him bring with him a hundred gunners,
 And rank riders let them be;
Let them be of the rankest riders
 That be to be found in that country.

"The best and worst and all in like,
 Bid him clothe them in one livery;
And for his men green is the best,
 And green now let their liveries be.   300

"And clothe himself in scarlet red,
  That is so seemly for to see;
For scarlet is a fair colour,
  And pleasant in a woman's ee."

What the lady said, John Stewart writ;
  To Argyle Castle sent it he;
His bag and his dish and showing horn
  Unto three beggars he gave them all three.

And when Willie Stewart saw the letter,
  Forth of care-bed then lope he;   310
He thought himself as lusty and sound
  As any man in that country.

He mustered together his merrymen all,
  He mustered them so lovingly;
He thought he had had scarce half a hundred,
  Then had he eleven score and three.

He chose forth a hundred of the best
  That were to be found in that company,
And presently they took their horse,
  And to Martingsdale posted he.   320

And when he came to Martingsdale,
  He found his love staying there truly;
For she was a lady true of love,
  And was there by the sun was a quarter high.

She kissed William Stewart and his brother John,
  So did she part of his merry men.
"If the churl thy father he were here,
  He should not have thee back again!"

They sent for the priest, they sent for the clerk,
  And they were married there with speed;   330
William took the lady home with him,
  And they lived together long time indeed.

And when twelve months had come and gone,
  The lady then she bore a child;
They sent John Stewart to the Earl of Mar
  To come and christen the barne so mild.

"I had rather make thee Earl of Mar,
  And marry my daughter unto thee;
For by my faith," says the Earl of Mar,
  "Her marriage is marred in our country."   340

"If this be so," then says John Stewart,
  "A marriage soon that thou shalt see;
For my brother William, my father's heir,
  Shall marry thy daughter before thine eye."

They sent for priest, they sent for clerk,
  And married there they were with speed;
And William Stewart is Earl of Mar,
  And his father-in-law dwells with him indeed.

BEWICK AND GRAHAME

Old Grahame he is to Carlisle gone,
  Where Sir Robert Bewick there met he;
In arms to the wine they are gone,
  And drank till they were both merry.

Old Grahame he took up the cup,
  And said, "Brother Bewick, here's to thee,
And here's to our two sons at home,
  For they live best in our country."

"Nay, were thy son as good as mine,
  And of some books could he but read,   10
With sword and buckler by his side,
  To see how he could save his head;

"They might have been call'd two bold brethren
  Where ever they did go or ride;
They might have been call'd two bold brethren,
  They might have crack'd the Border-side.

"Thy son is bad, and is but a lad,
  And bully to my son cannot be;
For my son Bewick can both write and read,
  And sure I am that cannot he."   20

"I put him to school, but he would not learn,
  I bought him books but he would not read;
But my blessing he's never have
  Till I see how his hand can save his head."

Old Grahame called for an account,
  And he ask'd what was for to pay;
There he paid a crown, so it went round,
  Which was all for good wine and hay.

Old Grahame is into the stable gone,
  Where stood thirty good steeds and three;   30
He's taken his own steed by the head,
  And home rode he right wantonly.

When he came home, there did he espy
  A loving sight to spy or see,
There did he espy his own three sons,
  Young Christy Grahame, the foremost was he.

There did he espy his own three sons,
  Young Christy Grahame, the foremost was he;
"Where have you been all day, father,
  That no counsel you would take by me?"   40

"Nay, I have been in Carlisle town,
  Where Sir Robert Bewick there met me;
He said thou was bad, and call'd thee a lad,
  And a baffled man by thou I be.

"He said thou was bad, and call'd thee a lad,
  And bully to his son cannot be;
For his son Bewick can both write and read,
  And sure I am that cannot thee.

"I put thee to school, but thou would not learn,
  I bought thee books, but thou would not read; 50
But my blessing thou's never have
  Till I see with Bewick thou can save thy head."

"Oh, pray forbear, my father dear;
  That ever such a thing should be!
Shall I venture my body in field to fight
  With a man that's faith and troth to me?"

"What's that thou sayst, thou limmer loon?
  Or how dare thou stand to speak to me?
If thou do not end this quarrel soon,
  Here is my glove, thou shalt fight me."   6ɔ

Christy stoop'd low unto the ground,
  Unto the ground, as you'll understand;
"O father, put on your glove again,
  The wind hath blown it from your hand."

"What's that thou sayst, thou limmer loon?
  Or how dare thou stand to speak to me?
If thou do not end this quarrel soon,
  Here is my hand, thou shalt fight me."

Christy Grahame is to his chamber gone,
  And for to study, as well might be,   70
Whether to fight with his father dear,
  Or with his bully Bewick he.

"If it be my fortune my bully to kill,
  As you shall boldly understand,
In every town that I ride through,
  They'll say, There rides a brotherless man!

"Nay, for to kill my bully dear,
  I think it will be a deadly sin;
And for to kill my father dear,
  The blessing of heaven I ne'er shall win.   80

"O give me your blessing, father," he said,
  "And pray well for me for to thrive;
If it be my fortune my bully to kill,
  I swear I'll ne'er come home alive."

He put on his back a good plate-jack,
  And on his head a cap of steel,
With sword and buckler by his side;
  O gin he did not become them well!

"O fare thee well, my father dear!
  And fare thee well, thou Carlisle town!   90
If it be my fortune my bully to kill,
  I swear I'll ne'er eat bread again."

Now we'll leave talking of Christy Grahame,
  And talk of him again belive;
But we will talk of bonny Bewick,
  Where he was teaching his scholars five.

Now when he had learn'd them well to fence,
  To handle their swords without any doubt,
He's taken his own sword under his arm,
  And walk'd his father's close about.   100

He look'd between him and the sun,
  To see what farleys he could see;
There he spy'd a man with armour on,
  As he came riding over the lee.

"I wonder much what man yon be
  That so boldly this way does come;
I think it is my nighest friend,
  I think it is my bully Grahame.

"O welcome, O welcome, bully Grahame!
  O man, thou art my dear, welcome!   110
O man, thou art my dear, welcome!
  For I love thee best in Christendom."

"Away, away, O bully Bewick,
  And of thy bullyship let me be!
The day is come I never thought on;
  Bully, I'm come here to fight with thee."

"O no! not so, O bully Grahame!
  That e'er such a word should spoken be!
I was thy master, thou was my scholar;
  So well as I have learned thee."   120

"My father he was in Carlisle town,
  Where thy father Bewick there met he;
He said I was bad, and he call'd me a lad,
  And a baffled man by thou I be."

"Away, away, O bully Grahame,
  And of all that talk, man, let us be!
We'll take three men of either side
  To see if we can our fathers agree."

"Away, away, O bully Bewick,
  And of thy bullyship let me be!   130
But if thou be a man, as I trow thou art,
  Come over this ditch and fight with me."

"O no, not so, my bully Grahame!
  That e'er such a word should spoken be!
Shall I venture my body in field to fight
  With a man that's faith and troth to me?"

"Away, away, O bully Bewick,
  And of all that care, man, let us be!
If thou be a man, as I trow thou art,
  Come over this ditch and fight with me."   140

"Now, if it be my fortune thee, Grahame, to kill,
  As God's will's, man, it all must be:
But if it be my fortune thee, Grahame, to kill,
  'Tis home again I'll never gae."

"Thou art then of my mind, bully Bewick,
  And sworn-brethren will we be;
If thou be a man, as I trow thou art,
  Come over this ditch and fight with me."

He flang his cloak from off his shoulders,
  His psalm-book out of his hand flang he,   150
He clapp'd his hand upon the hedge,
  And o'er lap he right wantonly.

When Grahame did see his bully come,
  The salt tear stood long in his eye;
"Now needs must I say that thou art a man,
  That dare venture thy body to fight with me.

"Now I have a harness on my back;
  I know that thou hath none on thine;
But as little as thou hath on thy back,
  Sure as little shall there be on mine."   160

He flang his jack from off his back,
  His steel cap from his head flang he;
He's taken his sword into his hand,
  He's tied his horse unto a tree.

Now they fell to it with two broad swords,
   For two long hours fought Bewick and he;
Much sweat was to be seen on them both,
   But never a drop of blood to see.

Now Grahame gave Bewick an ackward stroke,
   An ackward stroke surely struck he;   170
He struck him now under the left breast,
   Then down to the ground as dead fell he.

"Arise, arise, O bully Bewick,
   Arise, and speak three words to me!
Whether this be thy deadly wound,
   Or God and good surgeons will mend thee."

"O horse, O horse, O bully Grahame,
   And pray do get thee far from me!
Thy sword is sharp, it hath wounded my heart,
   And so no further can I gae.   180

"O horse, O horse, O bully Grahame,
   And get thee far from me with speed!
And get thee out of this country quite,
   That none may know who's done the deed."

"O if this be true, my bully dear,
   The words that thou dost tell to me,
The vow I made, and the vow I'll keep;
   I swear I'll be the first to die."

Then he stuck his sword in a moudie-hill,
   Where he lap thirty good foot and three;   190
First he bequeathed his soul to God,
   And upon his own sword-point lap he.

Now Grahame he was the first that died,
  And then came Robin Bewick to see;
"Arise, arise, O son," he said,
  "For I see thou's won the victory.

"Arise, arise, O son," he said,
  "For I see thou's won the victory."
"Father, could ye not drunk your wine at home,
  And letten me and my brother be?   200

"Nay, dig a grave both low and wide,
  And in it us two pray bury;
But bury my bully Grahame on the sun-side,
  For I'm sure he's won the victory."

Now we'll leave talking of these two brethren,
  In Carlisle town where they lie slain,
And talk of these two good old men,
  Where they were making a pitiful moan.

With that bespoke now Robin Bewick;
  "O man, was I not much to blame?   210
I have lost one of the liveliest lads
  That ever was bred unto my name."

With that bespoke my good lord Grahame;
  "O man, I have lost the better block;
I have lost my comfort and my joy,
  I have lost my key, I have lost my lock.

"Had I gone through all Ladderdale,
  And forty horse had set on me,
Had Christy Grahame been at my back,
  So well as he would guarded me."   220

I have no of more my song to sing,
   But two or three words to you I'll name;
But 'twill be talk'd in Carlisle town
   That these two old men were all the blame.

DICK O' THE COW

Now Liddisdale has long lain in,
   There is no riding there at a';
Their horse is growing so lidder and fatt
   That are lazie in the sta'.

Then Johnie Armstrong to Willie can say,
   "Billie, a riding then will we;
England and us has been long at a feed;
   Perhaps we may hitt of some bootie."

Then they're com'd on to Hutton Hall,
   They rade that proper place about;   10
But the laird he was the wiser man,
   For he had left nae gear without.

Then he had left nae gear to steal,
   Except six sheep upon a lee;
Says Johnie, "I'd rather in England die,
   Before their six sheep gaed to Liddisdale with me.

"But how call'd they the man we last with mett,
   Billie, as we came over the know?"
"That same he is an innocent fool,
   And some men calls him Dick o' the Cow."   20

"That fool has three as good kine of his own
   As is in a' Cumberland, billie," quoth he;
"Betide my life, betide my death,
   These three kine shall go to Liddisdale with me."

Then they're com'd on to the poor fool's house,
   And they have broken his walls so wide;
They have loosed out Dick o' the Cow's kine three,
   And ta'en three co'erlets off his wife's bed.

Then on the morn, when the day grew light,
   The shouts and crys rose loud and high;   30
"Hold thy tongue, my wife," he says,
   "And of thy crying let me bee.

"Hald thy tongue, my wife," he says,
   "And of thy crying let me bee,
And ay that where thou wants a kow,
   Good sooth that I shall bring thee three."

Then Dick's com'd on to lord and master,
   And I wot a drearie fool was he;
"Hald thy tongue, my fool," he says,
   "For I may not stand to jest with thee."   40

"Shame speed a' your jesting, my lord," quo' Dickie,
   "For nae such jesting 'grees with me;
Liddisdale has been in my house this last night,
   And they have ta'en my three kine from me.

"But I may nae langer in Cumberland dwell,
   To be your poor fool and your leal,
Unless ye give me leave, my lord,
   To go to Liddisdale and steal."

"To give thee leave, my fool," he says,
  "Thou speaks against mine honour and me;   50
Unless thou give me thy troth and thy right hand,
  Thou'l steal frae nane but them that sta' from thee."

"There is my troth and my right hand;
  My head shall hing on Hairibie,
I'll never cross Carlisle sands again,
  If I steal frae a man but them that sta' frae me."

Dickie has ta'en leave at lord and master,
  And I wot a merrie fool was he;
He has bought a bridle and a pair of new spurs,
  And has packed them up in his breek-thigh.   60

Then Dickie's come on for Puddinburn,
  Even as fast as he may drie;
Dickie's come on for Puddinburn,
  Where there was thirty Armstrongs and three.

"What's this com'd on me!" quo' Dickie,
  "What mickle wae's this happen'd on me,
Where here is but ae innocent fool,
  And there is thirty Armstrongs and three!"

Yet he's com'd up to the hall among them all;
  So wel he became his courtesie;   70
"Well may ye be, my good Laird's Jock,
  But the deil bless all your companie!

"I'm come to plain of your man Fair Johnie Arm-
    strong,
  And syne his billie Willie," quo' he;
"How they have been in my house this last night,
  And they have ta'en my three kye frae me."

Quo' Johnie Armstrong, "We'll him hang;"
  "Nay," then quo' Willie, "we'll him slae;
We'll nit him in a four-nooked sheet,
  Give him his burden of batts, and let him gae." 80

Then up bespake the good Laird's Jock,
  The best falla in the companie;
"Sit thy way down a little while, Dickie,
  And a piece of thine own cow's hough I'll give to
    thee."

But Dickie's heart it grew so great
  That never a bit of it he dought to eat;
But Dickie was ware of ane auld peat-house,
  Where there all the night he thought for to sleep.

Then Dickie was ware of that auld peat-house,
  Where there all the night he thought for to lie; 90
And a' the prayers the poor fool pray'd was,
  "I wish I had a mense for my own three kye!"

Then it was the use of Puddinburn,
  And the house of Mangertoun, all hail!
These that came not at the first call
  They got no more meat till the next meal.

The lads, that hungry and aevery was,
  Above the door-head they flang the key.
Dickie took good notice to that;
  Says, "There's a bootie yonder for me."   100

Then Dickie's gane into the stable,
  Where there stood thirty horse and three;
He has ty'd them a' with St Mary knot,
  All these horse but barely three.

He has ty'd them a' with St Mary knot,
  All these horse but barely three;
He has loupen on one, taken another in his hand,
  And out at the door and gane is Dickie.

Then on the morn, when the day grew light,
  The shouts and cries rose loud and high;   110
"What's that thief?" quo' the good Laird's Jock,
  "Tel me the truth and the verity.

"What's that thief?" quo' the good Laird's Jock,
  "See unto me ye do not lie."
"Dick o' the Cow has been in the stable this last night,
  And has my brother's horse and mine frae me."

"Ye wad never be tell'd it," quo' the Laird's Jock,
  "Have ye not found my tales fu' leal?
Ye wad never out of England bide,
  Till crooked and blind and a' wad steal."   120

"But will thou lend me thy bay?" Fair Johnie
    Armstrong can say,
  "There's nae horse loose in the stable but he;
And I'll either bring ye Dick o' the Cow again,
  Or the day is come that he must die."

"To lend thee my bay," the Laird's Jock can say,
  "He's both worth gold and good monie;
Dick o' the Cow has away twa horse,
  I wish no thou should make him three."

He has ta'en the Laird's jack on his back,
  The twa-handed sword that hang leugh by his
    thigh;   130
He has ta'en the steel cap on his head,
  And on is he to follow Dickie.

Then Dickie was not a mile off the town,
   I wot a mile but barely three,
Till John Armstrong has o'erta'en Dick o' the Cow,
   Hand for hand on Cannobie lee.

"Abide thee, bide now, Dickie, then,
   The day is come that thou must die."
Dickie looked o'er his left shoulder,
   "Johnie, has thou any mo in thy company?   140

"There is a preacher in our chapell,
   And a' the lee-lang day teaches he;
When day is gane, and night is come,
   There's never a word I mark but three.

"The first and second's Faith and Conscience,
   The third is, Johnie, Take heed of thee!
But what faith and conscience had thou, traitor,
   When thou took my three kye frae me?

"And when thou had ta'en my three kye,
   Thou thought in thy heart thou was no well sped; 150
But thou sent thy billie Willie o'er the know,
   And he took three co'erlets off my wife's bed."

Then Johnie let a spear fa' leugh by his thigh,
   Thought well to run the innocent through,
But the powers above was more than his,
   He ran but the poor fool's jerkin through.

Together they ran or ever they blan;
   This was Dickie the fool, and he;
Dickie could not win to him with the blade of the
     sword,
   But he fell'd him with the plummet under the eye. 160

Now Dickie has fell'd Fair Johnie Armstrong,
  The prettiest man in the south country;
"Gramercie," then can Dickie say,
  "I had twa horse, thou has made me three."

He has ta'en the laird's jack off his back,
  The twa-handed sword that hang leugh by his thigh;
He has ta'en the steel cap off his head;
  "Johnie, I'll tell my master I met with thee."

When Johnie waken'd out of his dream,
  I wot a dreary man was he;   170
"Is thou gane now, Dickie, then?
  The shame gae in thy company!

"Is thou gane now, Dickie, then?
  The shame go in thy companie!
For if I should live this hundred year,
  I shall never fight with a fool after thee."

Then Dickie comed home to lord and master,
  Even as fast as he may drie.
"Now, Dickie, I shall neither eat meat nor drink
  Till high hanged that thou shall be!"   180

"The shame speed the liars, my lord!" quo' Dickie,
  "That was no the promise ye made to me;
For I'd never gane to Liddisdale to steal
  Till that I sought my leave at thee."

"But what gart thou steal the Laird's Jock's horse?
  And, limmer, what gart thou steal him?" quo' he;
"For lang might thou in Cumberland dwelt
  Or the Laird's Jock had stoln ought frae thee."

"Indeed I wot ye lee'd, my lord,
    And even so loud as I hear ye lie;   190
I wan him frae his man, Fair Johnie Armstrong,
    Hand for hand on Cannobie lee.

"There's the jack was on his back,
    The twa-handed sword that hung leugh by his
        thigh;
There's the steel cap was on his head;
    I have a' these tokens to let you see."

"If that be true thou to me tells
    (I trow thou dare not tell a lie),
I'll give thee twenty pound for the good horse,
    Well tell'd in thy cloak-lap shall be.   200

"And I'll give thee one of my best milk-kye
    To maintain thy wife and children three;
And that may be as good, I think,
    As ony twa o' thine might be."

"The shame speed the liars, my lord!" quo' Dickie;
    "Trow ye ay to make a fool of me?
I'll either have thirty pound for the good horse,
    Or else he's gae to Mattan fair wi' me."

Then he has given him thirty pound for the good
        horse,
    All in gold and good monie;   210
He has given him one of his best milk-kye
    To maintain his wife and children three.

Then Dickie's come down through Carlisle town,
    Even as fast as he may drie.
The first of men that he with met
    Was my lord's brother, Bailiff Glazenberrie.

S.   9

"Well may ye be, my good Ralph Scrupe!"
  "Welcome, my brother's fool!" quo' he;
"Where did thou get Fair Johnie Armstrong's horse?"
  "Where did I get him but steal him," quo' he. 220

"But will thou sell me Fair Johnie Armstrong's horse?
  And, billie, will thou sell him to me?"
"Ay, and thou tell me the monie on my cloak-lap,
  For there's not one farthing I'll trust thee."

"I'll give thee fifteen pound for the good horse,
  Well told on thy cloak-lap shall be;
And I'll give thee one of my best milk-kye
  To maintain thy wife and thy children three."

"The shame speed the liars, my lord!" quo' Dickie,
  "Trow ye ay to make a fool of me?   230
I'll either have thirty pound for the good horse,
  Or else he's to Mattan Fair with me."

He has given him thirty pound for the good horse,
  All in gold and good monie;
He has given him one of his best milk-kye
  To maintain his wife and children three.

Then Dickie lap a loup on high,
  And I wot a loud laughter leugh he;
"I wish the neck of the third horse were broken,
  For I have a better of my own, and onie better
    can be."   240

Then Dickie com'd hame to his wife again.
  Judge ye how the poor fool he sped!
He has given her three score of English pounds
  For the three auld co'erlets was ta'en off her bed.

"Hae, take thee there twa as good kye,
    I trow, as all thy three might be;
And yet here is a white-footed nag,
    I think he'll carry both thee and me.

"But I may no langer in Cumberland dwell;
    The Armstrongs they'll hang me high."   250
But Dickie has ta'en leave at lord and master,
    And Burgh under Stanemuir there dwells Dickie.

JOHN O' THE SIDE

Peter o' Whitfield he hath slain,
    And John o' Side, he is ta'en,
And John is bound both hand and foot,
    And to the New-castle he is gane.

But tidings came to the Sybil o' the Side,
    By the water-side as she ran;
She took her kirdle by the hem,
    And fast she run to Mangerton.

[When she came into the hall,]
    The lord was set down at his meat;   10
When these tidings she did him tell,
    Never a morsel might he eat.

But lords they wrung their fingers white,
    Ladies did pull themselves by the hair,
Crying "Alas and welladay!
    For John o' the Side we shall never see mair.

"But we 'll go sell our droves of kine,
  And after them our oxen sell,
And after them our troops of sheep,
  But we will loose him out of the New Castell."   20

But then bespake him Hobby Noble,
  And spoke these words wondrous high;
Says, "Give me five men to myself,
  And I 'll fetch John o' the Side to thee."

"Yea, thou 'st have five, Hobby Noble,
  Of the best that are in this country;
I 'll give thee five thousand, Hobby Noble,
  That walk in Tyvidale truly."

"Nay, I 'll have but five," says Hobby Noble,
  "That shall walk away with me;   30
We will ride like no men of war,
  But like poor badgers we will be."

They stuffed up all their bags with straw,
  And their steeds barefoot must be;
"Come on, my brethren," says Hobby Noble,
  "Come on your ways, and go with me."

And when they came to Culerton ford,
  The water was up, they could it not go;
And then they were ware of a good old man,
  How his boy and he were at the plough.   40

"But stand you still," says Hobby Noble,
  "Stand you still here at this shore,
And I will ride to yonder old man,
  And see where the gate it lies o'er.

"But Christ you save, father!" quoth he,
  "Christ both you save and see!
Where is the way over this ford?
  For Christ's sake tell it me."

"But I have dwelled here three score year,
  So have I done three score and three;   50
I never saw man nor horse go o'er,
  Except it were a horse of tree."

"But fare thou well, thou good old man!
  The devil in hell I leave with thee,
No better comfort here this night
  Thou gives my brethren here and me."

But when he came to his brether again,
  And told this tidings full of woe,
And then they found a well-good gate
  They might ride o'er by two and two.   60

And when they were come over the ford,
  All safe gotten at the last,
"Thanks be to God!" says Hobby Noble,
  "The worst of our peril is past."

And then they came into Howbrame wood,
  And there then they found a tree,
And cut it down then by the root;
  The length was thirty foot and three.

And four of them did take the plank,
  As light as it had been a flea,   70
And carried it to the New Castle,
  Where as John o' Side did lie.

And some did climb up by the walls,
   And some did climb up by the tree,
Until they came up to the top of the castle,
   Where John made his moan truly.

He said, "God be with thee, Sybil o' the Side!
   My own mother thou art," quoth he;
"If thou knew this night I were here,
   A woe woman then wouldst thou be.   80

"And fare you well, Lord Mangerton!
   And ever I say God be with thee!
For if you knew this night I were here,
   You would sell your land for to loose me.

"And fare thou well, Much, Miller's son!
   Much, Miller's son, I say;
Thou has been better at mirk midnight
   Than ever thou was at noon o' the day.

"And fare thou well, my good lord Clough!
   Thou art thy father's son and heir;   90
Thou never saw him in all thy life
   But with him durst thou break a spear.

"We are brothers childer nine or ten,
   And sisters children ten or eleven;
We never came to the field to fight
   But the worst of us was counted a man."

But then bespake him Hobby Noble,
   And spake these words unto him;
Says, "Sleepest thou, wakest thou, John o' the Side,
   Or art thou this castle within?"   100

"But who is there," quoth John o' the Side,
  "That knows my name so right and free?"
"I am a bastard-brother of thine;
  This night I am comen for to loose thee."

"Now nay, now nay," quoth John o' the Side,
  "It fears me sore that will not be,
For a peck of gold and silver," John said,
  "In faith this night will not loose me."

But then bespake him Hobby Noble,
  And till his brother thus said he;   110
Says, "Four shall take this matter in hand,
  And two shall tent our geldings free."

Four did break one door without,
  Then John brake five himsel';
But when they came to the iron door,
  It smote twelve upon the bell.

"It fears me sore," said Much, the Miller,
  "That here taken we all shall be;"
"But go away, brethren," said John o' Side,
  "For ever alas! this will not be."   120

"But fie upon thee!" said Hobby Noble;
  "Much, the Miller, fie upon thee!
It sore fears me," said Hobby Noble,
  "Man that thou wilt never be."

But then he had Flanders files two or three,
  And he filed down that iron door,
And took John out of the New Castle,
  And said "Look thou never come here more!"

When he had him forth of the New Castle,
  "Away with me, John, thou shalt ride."   130
But ever alas! it could not be,
  For John could neither sit nor stride.

But then he had sheets two or three,
  And bound John's bolts fast to his feet,
And set him on a well-good steed,
  Himself on another by him set.

Then Hobby Noble smiled and lough,
  And spoke these words in mickle pride;
"Thou sits so finely on thy gelding
  That, John, thou rides like a bride."   140

And when they came thorough Howbrame town,
  John's horse there stumbled at a stane;
"Out and alas!" cried Much, the Miller,
  "John, thou'll make us all be ta'en."

"But fie upon thee!" says Hobby Noble,
  "Much, the Miller, fie on thee!
I know full well," says Hobby Noble,
  "Man that thou wilt never be."

And when they came into Howbrame wood,
  He had Flanders files two or three   150
To file John's bolts beside his feet,
  That he might ride more easily.

Says "John, now leap over a steed!"
  And John then he lope over five.
"I know well," says Hobby Noble,
  "John, thy fellow is not alive."

Then he brought him home to Mangerton;
  The lord then he was at his meat;
But when John o' the Side he there did see,
  For fain he could no more eat.   160

He says " Blest be thou, Hobby Noble,
  That ever thou wast man born!
Thou hast fetched us home good John o' the Side,
  That was now clean from us gone."

SIR HUGH IN THE GRIME

Good Lord John is a hunting gone,
  Over the hills and dales so fair,
For to take Sir Hugh in the Grime,
  For stealing of the bishop's mare.

Hugh in the Grime was taken then
  And carried to Carlisle town;
The merry women came out amain,
  Saying "The name of Grime shall never go down."

O then a jury of women was brought,
  Of the best that could be found;   10
Eleven of them spoke all at once,
  Saying "The name of Grime shall never go down."

And then a jury of men was brought,
  More the pity for to be!
Eleven of them spoke all at once,
  Saying "Hugh in the Grime, you are guilty."

Hugh in the Grime was cast to be hang'd,
  Many of his friends did for him lack;
For fifteen foot in the prison he did jump,
  With his hands tied fast behind his back.   20

Then bespoke our good Lady Ward,
  As she set on the bench so high;
"A peck of white pennys I'll give to my lord,
  If he'll grant Hugh Grime to me.

"And if it be not full enough,
  I'll stroke it up with my silver fan;
And if it be not full enough,
  I'll heap it up with my own hand."

"Hold your tongue now, Lady Ward,
  And of your talkitive let it be!   30
There is never a Grime came in this court
  That at thy bidding shall saved be."

Then bespoke our good Lady Moor,
  As she sat on the bench so high;
"A yoke of fat oxen I'll give to my lord,
  If he'll grant Hugh Grime to me."

"Hold your tongue now, good Lady Moor,
  And of your talkitive let it be!
There is never a Grime came to this court
  That at thy bidding saved shall be."   40

Sir Hugh in the Grime look'd out of the door,
  With his hand out of the bar;
There he spy'd his father dear,
  Tearing of his golden hair.

"Hold your tongue, good father dear,
   And of your weeping let it be!
For if they bereave me of my life,
   They cannot bereave me of the heavens so high."

Sir Hugh in the Grime look'd out at the door;
   Oh, what a sorry heart had he!   50
There he spy'd his mother dear,
   Weeping and wailing "Oh, woe is me!"

"Hold your tongue now, mother dear,
   And of your weeping let it be!
For if they bereave me of my life,
   They cannot bereave me of heaven's fee.

"I'll leave my sword to Johnny Armstrong,
   That is made of metal so fine,
That when he comes to the border-side
   He may think of Hugh in the Grime."   60

THE BRAES OF YARROW

"I dreamed a dreary dream this night,
   That fills my heart wi' sorrow;
I dreamed I was pouing the heather green
   Upon the braes of Yarrow.

"O true-luve mine, stay still and dine,
   As ye ha' done before, O;"
"O I'll be hame by hours nine,
   And frae the braes of Yarrow."

"I dreamed a dreary dream this night,
  That fills my heart wi' sorrow;   10
I dreamed my luve came headless hame,
  O frae the braes of Yarrow!

"O true-luve mine, stay still and dine,
  As ye ha' done before, O;"
"O I'll be hame by hours nine,
  And frae the braes of Yarrow."

"O are ye going to hawk," she says,
  "As ye ha' done before, O?
Or are ye going to wield your brand,
  Upon the braes of Yarrow?"   20

"O I am not going to hawk," he says,
  "As I have done before, O,
But for to meet your brother John,
  Upon the braes of Yarrow."

As he gaed down yon dowy den,
  Sorrow went him before, O;
Nine well-wight men lay waiting him,
  Upon the braes of Yarrow.

"I have your sister to my wife,
  Ye think me an unmeet marrow;   30
But yet one foot will I never flee
  Now frae the braes of Yarrow."

Then four he kill'd and five did wound,
  That was an unmeet marrow!
And he had weel nigh won the day
  Upon the braes of Yarrow.

But a cowardly loon came him behind,
　　Our Lady lend him sorrow!
And wi' a rapier pierced his heart,
　　And laid him low on Yarrow.　　　　　　40

Now Douglas to his sister's gane,
　　Wi' meikle dule and sorrow:
"Gae to your luve, sister," he says,
　　"He's sleeping sound on Yarrow."

As she went down yon dowy den,
　　Sorrow went her before, O;
She saw her true-love lying slain
　　Upon the braes of Yarrow.

She swooned thrice upon his breast
　　That was her dearest marrow;　　　　　　50
Said, "Ever alas, and wae the day
　　Thou went'st frae me to Yarrow!"

She kist his mouth, she kaimed his hair,
　　As she had done before, O;
She wiped the blood that trickled doun
　　Upon the braes of Yarrow.

Her hair it was three quarters lang,
　　It hang baith side and yellow;
She tied it round her white hause-bane,
　　And tint her life on Yarrow.　　　　　　60

SIR PATRICK SPENCE

The king sits in Dumferling toune,
  Drinking the blude-reid wine:
"O whare will I get a guid sailor,
  To sail this schip of mine?"

Up and spake an eldern knicht,
  Sat at the king's richt knee.
"Sir Patrick Spence is the best sailor
  That sails upon the sea."

The king has written a braid letter,
  And sign'd it wi' his hand,   10
And sent it to Sir Patrick Spence,
  Was walking on the sand.

The first line that Sir Patrick read,
  A loud lauch lauched he;
The next line that Sir Patrick read,
  The teir blinded his ee.

"O wha is this has done this deid,
  This ill deid done to me?
To send me out this time o' the yeir,
  To sail upon the sea!   20

"Make haste, make haste, my merry men all,
  Our guid schip sails the morne!"
"O say na sae, my master deir,
  For I feir a deadlie storme.

"Late, late yestreen I saw the new moone
  Wi' the auld moone in hir arme,
And I feir, I feir, my deir master,
  That we will cum to harme."

O our Scots nobles wer richt laith
  To weet their cork-heil'd schoone;   30
But lang ere a' the play were play'd,
  Their hats they swam aboone.

O lang, lang may their ladies sit
  Wi' their fans into their hand
Or ere they see Sir Patrick Spence
  Cum sailing to the land.

O lang, lang may the ladies stand,
  Wi' their gold kems in their hair,
Waiting for their ain deir lords,
  For they'll see them na mair.   40

Haf owre, haf owre to Aberdour,
  It's fiftie fadom deip,
And there lies guid Sir Patrick Spence,
  Wi' the Scots lords at his feit.

THE GARDENER

The gardener stands in his bower-door,
  With a primrose in his hand,
And by there came a leal maiden,
  As jimp's a willow wand.

"O lady, can you fancy me,
  For to be my bride?
You'll get a' the flowers in my garden
  To be to you a weed.

"The lily white shall be your smock,
  Becomes your body neat;   10
And your head shall be deck'd with jellyflower,
  And the primrose in your breast.

"Your gown shall be o' the sweet-william,
  Your coat o' camovine,
And your apron o' the salads neat,
  That taste baith sweet and fine.

"Your stockings shall be o' the broad kail-blade,
  That is baith broad and long;
And narrow, narrow at the coot,
  And broad, broad at the brawn.   20

"Your gloves shall be the marigold
  All glittering to your hand,
Well spread o'er wi' the blue blaewort,
  That grows in corn-land."

"O fare you well, young man," she says,
  "Farewell, and I bid adieu;
[O fare you well, young man," she says,
  For I cannot fancy you.]

"Since you 've provided a weed for me
  Among the summer flowers,   30
Then I 'll provide another for you
  Among the winter showers.

"The new-fallen snow to be your smock,
  Becomes your body neat;
And your head shall be decked with the eastern wind,
  And the cold rain on your breast."

THOMAS O' POTT

[PART I]

All you lords of Scotland fair,
  And ladies also bright of blee;
There is a lady amongst them all,
  Of her report you shall hear of me.

Of her beauty she is so bright,
  And of her colour so bright of blee;
She is daughter to the Lord Arundel,
  His heir-apparent for to be.

"I 'll see that bride," Lord Phenix says,
  "That is a lady of high degree,   10
And if I like her countenance well,
  The heir of all my land she 'st be."

To that lady fair lord Phenix came,
   And to that likesome dame said he;
"Now God thee save, my lady fair,
   The heir of all my land thou'st be."

"Leave off your suit," the lady said;
   "You are a lord of honour free;
You may get ladies enow at home,
   And I have a love in mine own country.   20

"I have a lover true of mine own,
   A serving-man of a small degree;
Thomas o' Pott it is his name;
   My first and last love he shall be."

"Gif Thomas o' Pott then be his name,
   I wot I ken him so readily;
I can spend forty pounds by week,
   And he cannot spend poundès three."

"God give you good of your gold," she said,
   "And also, sir, of your fee!   30
He was the first love that ever I had,
   And the last, sir, he shall be."

With that Lord Phenix was sore amoved;
   Unto her father then went he;
He told her father how it was proved
   How that his daughter's mind was set.

"Thou art my daughter," Lord Arundel said,
   "The heir of all my land to be;
Thou'st be bride to the Lord Phenix,
   Daughter, gif thou'll be heir to me."   40

For lack of her love this lady must lose,
  Her foolish wooing lay all aside;
The day is appointed and friends are agreed;
  She is forced to be the Lord Phenix bride.

With that the lady began to muse;
  A grieved woman, God wot, was she;
How she might Lord Phenix beguile,
  And scape unmarried from him that day.

She called to her her little foot-page,
  To Jack her boy, so tenderly;   50
Says, "Come thou hither, thou little foot-page,
  For indeed I dare trust none but thee.

"To Strawberry Castle, boy, thou must go,
  To Thomas Pott, thereas he can be,
And give him here this letter fair,
  And on Gilford Green bid him meet me.

"Look thou mark his countenance well,
  And his colour tell to me;
And hie thee fast and come again,
  And forty shillings I will give thee.   60

"For if he blushes in his face,
  Then in his heart he's sorry be;
Then let my father say what he will,
  For false to Potts I'll never be.

"And gif he smile then with his mouth,
  Then in his heart he'll merry be;
Then may he get him a love where he can,
  For small of his company my part shall be."

10—2

Then one while that the boy he went,
  Another while, God wot, ran he;   70
And when he came to Strawberry Castle,
  There Thomas Potts he see.

Then he gave him this letter fair,
  And when he began then for to read,
The boy had told him by word of mouth
  His love must be the Lord Phenix bride.

With that, Thomas Potts began to blush;
  The tearès trickled in his eye:
"Indeed this letter I cannot read,
  Nor never a word to see or spy.   80

"I pray thee, boy, to me thou'll be true,
  And here's five mark I will give thee;
And all these words thou must peruse
  And tell thy lady this from me.

"By faith and troth she is mine own,
  By some part of promise so it's be found;
Lord Phenix shall not have her, night nor day,
  Without he can win her with his hand.

"On Gilford Green I will her meet;
  And bid that lady for me pray,   90
For there I'll lose my life so sweet
  Or else the wedding I will stay."

Then back again the boy he went,
  As fast again as he could hie;
The lady met him five mile on the way:
  "Why hast thou stayed so long?" says she.

"Boy," said the lady, "thou art but young;
  To please my mind thou'll mock and scorn;
I will not believe thee on word of mouth
  Unless on this book thou wilt be sworn."   100

"Marry, by this book," the boy can say,
  "As Christ himself be true to me,
Thomas Potts could not his letter read
  For tearès trickling in his eye."

"If this be true," the lady said,
  "Thou bonny boy, thou tells to me,
Forty shillings I did thee promise,
  But here's ten pounds I'll give it thee.

"All my maids," the lady said,
  "That this day do wait on me,   110
We will fall down upon our knees;
  For Thomas Potts now pray will we.

"If his fortune be now for to win—
  We'll pray to Christ in Trinity—
I'll make him the flower of all his kin,
  For the Lord of Arundel he shall be."

[PART II]

Now let us leave talking of this lady fair,
  In her prayer good where she can be;
And I'll tell you how Thomas o' Pott
  For aid to his lord and master came he.   120

And when he came Lord Jocky before,
  He kneeled him low down on his knee.
Says, "Thou art welcome, Thomas Potts,
  Thou art always full of thy courtesy.

"Hast thou slain any of thy fellows,
  Or hast thou wrought me some villainy?"
"Sir, none of my fellows have I slain,
  Nor have I wrought you no villainy.

"But I have a love in Scotland fair,
  I doubt I must lose her through poverty;   130
If you will not believe me by word of mouth,
  Behold the letter she writ unto me!"

When Lord Jocky looked the letter upon,
  The tender words in it could be:
"Thomas Potts, take thou no care,
  Thou'st never lose her through poverty.

"Thou shalt have forty pounds a week,
  In gold and silver thou shalt row;
And Harby town I will thee allow
  As long as thou dost mean to woo.   140

"Thou shalt have forty of thy fellows fair,
  And forty horse to go with thee,
And forty spears of the best I have,
  And I myself in thy company."

"I thank you, master," said Thomas Potts,
  "Neither man nor boy shall go with me;
I would not for a thousand pounds
  Take one man in my company."

"Why, then, God be with thee, Thomas Potts!
  Thou art well known and proved for a man;   150
Look thou shed no guiltless blood,
  Nor never confound no gentleman.

"But look thou take with him some truce;
  Appoint a place of liberty;
Let him provide as well as he can,
  And as well provided thou shalt be."

And when Thomas Potts came to Gilford Green
  And walkèd there a little beside,
Then was he ware of the Lord Phenix
  And with him Lady Rosamond his bride.   160

Away by the bride rode Thomas o' Pott,
  But no word to her that he did say;
But when he came Lord Phenix before
  He gave him the right time of the day.

"O thou art welcome, Thomas o' Pott,
  Thou serving-man, welcome to me!
How fares thy lord and master at home,
  And all the ladies in thy country?"

"Sir, my lord and master is in good health,
  I wot I ken it so readily;—   170
I pray you, will you ride to an outside,
  A word or two to talk with me?

"You are a nobleman," said Thomas o' Pott;
  "And born a lord in Scotland free;
You may get ladies enow at home;
  You shall never take my love from me."

"Away, away, thou Thomas o' Pott!
  Thou serving-man, stand thou aside!
There's not a serving-man this day,
  I wot, can hinder me of my bride."   180

"If I be but a serving-man," said Thomas,
  "And you are a lord of honour free,
A spear or two with you I'll run
  Before I'll lose her thus cowardly."

"On Gilford Green I will thee meet,
  Nor man nor boy shall come with me."
"As I am a man," said Thomas o' Pott,
  "I'll have as few in my company."

With that, the wedding-day was stayed;
  The bride unmarried went home again;   190
Then to her maidens fast she lough,
  And in her heart she was full fain.

"But all my maids," the lady said,
  "That this day do wait on me,
We'll fall down again upon our knees;
  For Thomas o' Pott now pray will we.

"If his fortune be for to win—
  We'll pray to Christ in Trinity—
I'll make him the flower of all his kin,
  For the Lord of Arundel he shall be."   200

[PART III]

Now let us leave talking of this lady fair,
  In her prayers good where she can be;
I'll tell you the truth how Thomas o' Pott
  For aid to his lord again came he.

And when he came to Strawberry Castle,
  To try for his lady he had but one week;
Alack, for sorrow he cannot forbear,
  For four days then he fell sick.

With that, his master to him came;
   Says, "Prithee tell me without all doubt,   210
Whether hast thou gotten the bonny lady,
   Or thou maun gang the lady without?"

"Marry,·master, that matter is yet untried;
   Within two days tried must it be;
He is a lord, I am but a serving-man;
   I doubt I must lose her through poverty."

"Why, Thomas o' Pott, take thou no care,
   My former promises kept shall be;
As I am a lord in Scotland fair,
   Thou'st never lose her through poverty.   220

"Thou shalt have half my land a year,
   And that will raise thee many a pound;
Before thou shalt lose thy bonny lady
   Thou shalt drop angels with him to the ground.

"And thou shalt have forty of thy fellows fair,
   And forty horses to go with thee,
And forty spears of the best I have,
   And I myself in thy company."

"I thank you, master," said Thomas o' Pott;
   "But of one thing, sir, I would be fain;   230
If I should lose my bonny lady,
   How shall I increase your goods again?"

"Why, if thou win thy lady fair,
   Thou may well forth for to pay me;
If thou lose thy lady, thou hast loss enough,
   Not one penny will I ask thee."

"Master, you have thirty horses in hold,
　You keep them rank and royally;
Amongst them all there's one old horse
　This day would set my lady free.　　　　240

"That is a white, with a cut tail;
　Full sixteen years of age is he;
Gif you would lend me that old horse,
　Then I should get her easily."

"A foolish part," Lord Jocky said,
　"And a foolish part thou takes on thee;
Thou shalt have a better than ever he was,
　That forty pounds cost more nor he."

"O master, those horses ben wild and wicked,
　And little can skill of the old train;　　250
Gif I be out of my saddle cast,
　They ben so wild they'll never be ta'en.

"Let me have age, sober and wise;
　'Tis part of wisdom, you know it plain;
If I be out of my saddle cast,
　He'll either stand still or turn again."

"Thou shalt have that horse with all my heart,
　And my coat-plate of silver free,
And a hundred men to stand at thy back,
　For to fight if need shall be."　　　　260

"I thank you, master," said Thomas o' Pott;
　"Neither man nor boy shall go with me;
As you are a lord of honour born,
　Let none of my fellows know this of me.

"For if they wot of my going,
    I wot behind me they will not be;
Without you keep them under a lock,
    Upon that green I shall them see."

And when Thomas came to Gilford Green,
    And walkèd there some hourès three,   270
Then was he ware of the Lord Phenix,
    And four men in his company.

"You have broken your vow," said Thomas o' Pott,
    "Your vow that you made unto me;
You said you would come yourself alone,
    And you have brought more than two or three."

"These are my men," Lord Phenix said,
    "That every day do wait on me;
Gif any of these should at us stir,
    My spear should run through his body."   280

"I'll run no race," said Thomas o' Pott,
    "Till that this oath here made may be:
If the one of us be slain,
    The other forgiven that he may be."

"I'll make a vow," Lord Phenix says,
    "My men shall bear witness with thee;
Gif thou slay me at this time,
    No worse belovèd thou shalt be."

Then they turned their horses round about,
    To run the race more eagerly;   290
Lord Phenix he was stiff and stout,
    He has run Thomas quite through the thigh,

And bare Thomas out of his saddle fair;
  Upon the ground there he did lie.
He says, "For my life I do not care,
  But for the love of my lady.

"But shall I lose my lady fair?
  I thought she would have been my wife.
I pray thee, Lord Phenix, ride not away,
  For with thee I will lose my life."   300

Though Thomas o' Pott was a serving-man,
  He was also a physician good;
He clapped his hand upon his wound,
  With some kind of words he staunched the blood.

Then into his saddle again he leapt;
  The blood in his body began to warm;
He missed Lord Phenix body there,
  But ran him through the brawn of the arm,

And he bore him quite out of his saddle fair;
  Upon the ground there did he lie;   310
Says, "Prithee, Lord Phenix, rise up and fight,
  Or yield this lady sweet to me."

"To fight with thee I cannot stand;
  Nor for to fight I cannot, sure;
Thou hast run me through the brawn of the arm
  That with a spear I cannot endure.

"Thou'st have that lady with all my heart,
  Sith it was like never better to prove,
With never a nobleman this day,
  That will seek to take a poor man's love."   320

"Why then be of good cheer," says Thomas Potts,
  "Indeed your butcher I'll never be,
For I will come and staunch your blood,
  Gif any thanks you'll give to me."

As he was staunching the Phenix blood,
  Lord, in his heart he did rejoice!
"I'll never take lady of you thus,
  But here I'll give you another choice.

"Here is a lane of two miles long;
  At either end set we will be;   330
The lady shall sit us between;
  Her own choice shall set her free."

"If thou'll do so," Lord Phenix says,
  "Thomas o' Pott, as thou dost tell me,
Whether I get her or go without her,
  Forty pounds I will give thee."

And when the lady there can stand,
  A woman's mind that day to prove:
"Now by my faith," said this lady fair,
  "Thomas o' Pott shall have his love!"   340

Toward Thomas o' Pott the lady she went,
  To leap behind him hastily.
"Nay, abide awhile," said Lord Phenix,
  "For better yet provèd thou shalt be.

"Thou shalt stay here with all thy maids—
  In number with thee thou hast but three—
Thomas and I'll go behind yonder wall;
  There the one of us shall die."

But when they came behind the wall,
   The one would not the other nigh;   350
Lord Phenix he had given his word
   With Thomas o' Pott never to fight.

"Give me a choice," Lord Phenix says,
   "Thomas o' Pott, I do pray thee;
Let me go to yonder lady fair,
   To see whether she be true to thee."

And when he came that lady to,
   Unto that likesome dame said he:
"Now God thee save, thou lady fair,
   The heir of all my land thou'st be.   360

"For this Thomas I have him slain;
   He hath more than death-wounds two or three;
Thou art mine own lady," he said,
   "And married together we will be."

"If Thomas o' Pott this day thou have slain,
   Thou hast slain a better man than thee;
And I'll sell all the 'state of my land,
   But thou'st be hanged on a gallows-tree."

With that, the lady she fell in a swoon;
   A grievèd woman, I wot, was she;   370
Lord Phenix he was ready there,
   Took her in his arms most hastily.

"O lady sweet, and stand on thy feet!
   This day Thomas alive can be;
I'll send for thy father, Lord Arundel;
   And married together I will you see."

"I'll see that wedding," Lord Arundel said,
  "Of my daughter's love that is so fair,
And sith it will no better be,
  Of all my land he shall be the heir."   380

"Now all my maids," the lady said,
  "And ladies of England fair and free,
Change never your old love for no new,
  Nor never change for no poverty.

"For I had a lover true of my own,
  A serving-man of a small degree;
From Thomas o' Pott I'll turn his name,
  And the Lord of Arundel he shall be!"

NOTES

THE LORD OF LEARNE

This story of the young Lord of Learne (also called the Lord of Lorne, under which title the ballad is often referred to by the Elizabethan dramatists) and the false steward, is derived from a romance known as *Roswall and Lillian*, which must have been popular in the sixteenth and seventeenth centuries, and continued to be recited in verse form in Scotland until early in the nineteenth century. Sir Walter Scott remembered a person who "acquired the name of Roswall and Lillian, from singing that romance about the streets of Edinburgh," circa 1770.

The best-known of similar stories is the *Goose-girl* in Grimm's Fairy Tales.

The version of the ballad printed here is derived from the Percy Folio MS. (see Introduction, pp. 11—12), and was therefore written down about 1650.

24. **that.** This insertion of an apparently redundant or unnecessary *that* occurs often in this particular manuscript, and may be due to the dialect in which it is written. Cf. in this ballad ll. 30, 56, 278, 288, 393, &c. but notice that in many instances it is used in an optative sentence, exactly as it is used in Ireland to-day to express a wish (see the plays of J. M. Synge).

42. **and then.** This, again, is a redundant phrase. Cf. the *and* in early literature:

"When that I was *and* a little tiny boy,"

in the song sung by the Clown at the end of Shakespeare's *Twelfth Night*. See l. 110.

46. **Until,** unto.

47. **hend,** friendly, noble.

52. **mickle mere,** much more.

67. **He** is of course the steward.

76. **fain,** desirous.

s.   11

82. **lend,** grant.

89. **Do thou me off:** *do off* (otherwise contracted into *doff*, as *do on* into *don*)=*take off*. The *me* is called the ethic dative, as in "Kill me this knave," implying *for me*.

91. **cordivant,** made of leather from Cordova in Spain; also *cordwain.* A cordwainer is an old name for a shoemaker. See *Will Stewart and John,* 195.

91—2. Note the omission of the relative *which.* Cf. ll. 147—8, 375—6.

107. **him fro,** from him.

115. **Disaware** is the name adopted by Roswall in the romance.

122. **see,** protect. So often in this phrase.

130. **thou'st**=thou shalt.

141—4. This kind of remark in the first person is of constant occurrence in ballads, in places where a dramatist would simply mark a change of scene.

156. A proverb, meaning that too much may be given even for valuable things.

168. **Unseemly;** it was held to be not proper that those of low birth, like the steward, should sit at meat with the nobly-born.

172. **mend,** increase.

221. **fee,** wages.

238. **i-wis,** certainly.

266. **gelding,** a kind of horse.

284. **let,** stop.

289. We must understand that the steward had exacted an oath from the Lord of Learne that he would not reveal the truth about himself to anybody. He avoids doing so by speaking to the horse, knowing, of course, that the lady overhears him. This trick is a favourite one in folk-tales.

348. **Wroken,** avenged.

369. **light,** alighted. Cf. l. 178, *plight*=plighted.

393. **quest,** jury.

412. **sod,** soused; **lead,** a cauldron. A large pan or vat, used for salting meat, is still called a *salting-lead.*

416. **I-wis;** see note on l. 238. **curstly cumber,** savagely torture.

427—8. These and several other lines, it will be noticed, are too long for the ballad-metre; but this is no reason for altering them.

For further information, see my *Popular Ballads of the Olden Time,* Second Series, 182.

YOUNG BEKIE

There is a great number and variety of stories similar to this in many countries of Europe; but the English—or rather the Scottish—version has undoubtedly been grafted on to the legendary story of Gilbert Becket, the father of St Thomas. He is said to have been captured and imprisoned by a Saracen prince, named Admiraud, whose daughter set him free and then followed him to England, knowing no English save the words 'London' and 'Gilbert.' After much wandering and trouble, she found him and was married to him. But it must not be rashly imagined that 'Bekie' is derived from 'Becket'; the similarity of the names may account for the joining of the two stories, but 'Bekie' was probably the name of the hero of the ballad before contamination with the Becket-legend took place.

4. **fee**, pay, money.

10. **Burd**=maiden. Cf. *Fair Helen of Kirconnell*, 7.

12. **mane**, moan.

13. **borrow**, ransom, buy off.

20. **Linne**, an imaginary place, the stock-locality in ballads. Here we must suppose that it is young Bekie's home.

21—2. **but...ben**, out...in. The two words were originally prepositions, equivalent to *be-out* and *be-in*, the *be-* being identical with the prefix in *behind, beside, before*, &c. They then were used, especially in Scottish dialect, as adverbs both of rest and motion. Later they became substantives, so that a *but-and-ben* house means a house with an outer and an inner chamber. They are constantly used in conjunction in Scottish ballads.

27. **stown**=stolen.

31. **but an'**=and. **rottons**, rats.

38. **royal bone.** In early poetry, most saddles are described as being made of *roelle bone* (*rewel, rowel*, and other corruptions are found). It is not known exactly what *roelle* means, but a derivation from the French *rouelle* has been suggested—implying that the peak of the saddle was made of bone, rounded and polished.

40. *i.e.* one was named Hector.

43. **or**, ere, before.

52. **kensnae**, knows not.

55. **the Billy Blin** (= the Blind Man), the name of a benignant domestic spirit or demon, who appears only in a very few ballads. There are German and Dutch references to a similar spirit with a similar name.

63. **marys,** maids.

64. **thinking lang,** thinking it long, or tedious. Observe that burd Isbel would be bored, had she not 'twa marys' to keep her company and divert her.

85. **gid**=gaed, went.

101. **he** is the proud porter.

113. **bierly,** stately.

116. **We's be**=we shall be.

135. **ilka,** each.

137. This of course is spoken by young Bekie to the parents of the 'bierly bride,' who in the next verse naturally resent his jilting of their daughter.

See my *Popular Ballads*, First Series, 6.

THE TWA SISTERS OF BINNORIE

The story in this ballad has long been popular not only in England and Scotland, but in all Scandinavian countries. The name of the place or river Binnorie (which should be stressed on the second syllable to rhyme with 'story') has nothing to do with the ballad; it is part of an attached burden. Several Scottish versions have quite another burden.

1. **bour** (=bower) should be so pronounced as to rhyme approximately with *wooer*.

31. **jaw,** wave; *i.e.* threw her into the river.

43. **twinèd,** parted: **my world's make,** my earthly mate.

55. **garr'd me gang,** caused me to go.

61. We must suppose the miller's son to be speaking; he is actually mentioned in one version.

75. **bra'**=braw, brave.

93. **syne,** afterwards.

See also my *Popular Ballads*, First Series, 141.

KING ESTMERE

This ballad was rewritten by Bishop Percy from an older form preserved in his Folio MS., but he tore out the pages on which it was originally written, so that they are now missing.

3. **brether,** brothers; cf. *brethren.*

5—6. **tone...tother,** *i.e.* the one...the other.

18. **sheen,** beautiful.

21. **rede**, advise. King Estmere is speaking.

25. Adler is speaking.

29. **renisht**. The meaning and derivation of this word are unknown (see Introduction, p. 8). It probably means harnessed or accoutred.

32. **weeds**, clothes; as we speak of 'widow's weeds.'

36. **rearing himself**, standing.

38. **see**, protect. Cf. *The Lord of Learne*, 122, &c.

47. *i.e.* refused him.

50. **Mahound**, Mahomet. Charles Kingsley quotes this verse at the head of Chapter xv. of *Westward Ho!*

62. **pall**, fine cloth.

67. Notice omission of the relative.

78. **sped**, arranged.

84. **reave**, rob, deprive.

90. **doubt**, fear. See *Young Benjie*, 67.

93. **to your wife**: *to* = as; cf. 'take to wife.'

103. **scant**, scarcely.

106. **kempès**, knights, fighting-men. The word is derived from the same source as *champion*.

118. **I-wis**, surely, truly: **blan**, lingered.

136. My counsel shall be set up by you.

144. **gramary**, magic (French, *gramoire*, a conjuring-book).

148. **And-if** = if.

149—150. *i.e.* the herb will make black and brown the colour of that man who is white and red.

157. **fain**, desirous.

183. **Said**: *i.e.* the porter said. **And** = if.

189. **will**, desire.

195. It is quite in keeping with ancient custom for knights to ride into the hall, and stable their steeds beside the tables, but not for harpers.

198. **Bremor** is the name of "the king his son of Spain" = the son of the king of Spain.

203. **lither**, lazy.

215. **kempery-man**, fighting-man. Cf. 106.

218. **nigh**, approach.

231. **and**, if. Cf. 148, 183, &c.

232. **till**, entice.

235. **lough**, laughed.

366666666

OLD BALLADS

237. King Bremor is speaking.

243. **fit**, song, or part of a song. Ballads were sometimes divided into 'fits.'

244. **be**=been.

248. **ben**=are.

264. **Sowdan**, soldan, sultan. The name was given to any pagan king, and Bremor, we are told, ''lieveth on Mahound.'

270. **swithe**, quickly.

272. **stiff in stour**, staunch in fight (a ballad 'commonplace').

273. **can** is an auxiliary of the verb 'to be,' *can be* meaning *is*; thence *can* is often used as=to *does* or *do*, but is sometimes confused with *'gan*=*began*. Here **can bite**=*do bite*.

THE HEIR OF LINNE

This text is also from the Percy Folio, and will be found to contain characteristics of that manuscript. See *The Lord of Learne*, *Thomas o' Pott*, &c.

'Linne,' of course, is the town so dear to ballads, but any attempt to identify it (for example, with Lincoln or King's Lynn) is a waste of labour. See *Young Bekie*, 20.

There are Oriental stories—Arabic, Persian, Turkish, &c.—resembling (in part) this ballad; but in these the climax comes when the hero, in attempting to hang himself in despair, pulls down the ceiling to which the rope is fastened, and so reveals a hidden treasure.

8. **blin**, linger. See *King Estmere*, 118, &c.

14. **fee**, money. See *Lord of Learne*, 221.

17, 18. The Heir speaks.

19. John of the Scales speaks.

20. **a God's penny**=an 'earnest-penny,' a penny given to clinch a bargain.

36. Presumably a silver penny; but it is not clear what the use is of a brass or lead penny. Brass, however, may mean bronze or copper.

43. The order of the lines is corrupt. **rede**=advice.

49. **fere**, companion, friend.

54. **irk with**, weary of.

62. **unbethought him**=bethought him on, or bethought him of. This curious expression occurs only two or three times in the Folio MS. **bill**=paper, document.

70. **that** is superfluous; see note on *The Lord of Learne*, 24.

72. **in fere,** together. Lit. 'in company'; see 49.

75. **bags of bread** = a beggar's collecting bags.

80. **speer.** This is corrupt, and the meaning is not known. It has been conjectured that a 'speer' may have been a hole in the wall of a house through which visitors made inquiries (Scottish *speir*, to ask).

87. **trust me one shot.** *Shot* = reckoning, as in the phrase still in use, 'to pay the shot' = to pay the bill. The Heir asks credit for one occasion only.

103—4. *i.e.* cheaper by twenty pounds than its cost.

122. Some lines are lost here. It will be seen that a good deal of corruption has rather spoiled the arrangement and rhymes of this ballad.

BARBARA ALLAN

Although this ballad does not appear to be very old, and cannot be traced back beyond the seventeenth century, it has been widely popular, appealing to such different men as Samuel Pepys and Oliver Goldsmith. It is apparently, as Pepys calls it, "a little Scotch song." The tune is still well-known.

9. **hooly,** slowly.

10, 12. It has been suggested that **lying** and **dying** should be interchanged.

15. **ye 's** = you shall.

31. **jow,** stroke: **geid,** gave.

Further information will be found in my *Popular Ballads*, First Series, 150.

LORD RANDAL

This ballad illustrates several characteristics of popular literature. It is also known as *Lord Ronald, Lord Rendal, The Croodlin Doo*, and so on. Sir Walter Scott tried to identify the hero with Thomas Randolph (or Randal), Earl of Murray, who died at Musselburgh in 1332. But a similar story is found in many other lands; and the poisoning is usually done by means of snakes (rather than 'eels')— a common ancient way of poisoning. This ballad, moreover, is one of those that have been transferred at one time or another to America, where 'Lord Randal' has become corrupted into 'Tiranti.'

Notice that, simple as the ballad is, it is full of repetition; the whole story could be told in five questions and five answers:

> *Q.* "O where hae ye been?"
> *A.* "I hae been to the wild wood."
> *Q.* "Where gat ye your dinner?"
> *A.* "I dined wi' my true-love," etc.

Nor are we given any reason for the poisoning; Lord Randal's true-love may or may not have intended to poison him, but that is no concern of the ballad-singer's.

4, &c. **wald** = would.

11. **broo**, broth.

FAIR ANNIE OF ROUGH ROYAL

This ballad supplies us with a very good instance of the dramatic nature of the singing. The replies from inside the house (ll. 37—40, 45—48, 61—64) to Fair Annie's appeals, are spoken by Love Gregor's mother; but we do not know this in reading the ballad until we come to line 80, where we find that the lover has been asleep all night, and that it was his mother who feigned his voice in order to turn Fair Annie from the door.

French, German, and modern Greek ballads tell a similar story.

3. **jimp**, slender, graceful.

5. **kaim** = comb. In ancient times it was a kind act of courtesy to comb the hair of other people.

9. Presumably Fair Annie's mother is replying.

19. **maun gang** = must go.

39. **wile** = vile; **warlock**, wizard.

67. *i.e.* he raised himself up, rose up.

70. **gars me greet**, makes me weep.

76. **wan no in** = won not in. To *win in*, like to *win through*, implies to pass in or through in the face of opposition.

78. **dead** = death.

106. **neist** = next.

110. **die**: pronounce *dee* in the Scottish way, to rhyme with *me*.

Further information will be found in my *Popular Ballads*, First Series, 179.

THE GAY GOSHAWK

In this charming and happy ballad, a true-loving lady outwits her father by pretending to be dead, in order that she may escape from her home in England to her Scottish lover, who owns a useful goshawk. We need not remark that a goshawk cannot sing, much less speak; this does not matter to the ballad-singer!

1. **O well 's me o'** = *O well is it for me that I have*, or "it is a good thing for me to have a goshawk," etc.

5. The bird replies.

7. **couth**, speech, word.

20. **goud** = gold.

27. **he** is the goshawk.

29. **marys** = maids. See *Young Bekie*, 63.

31. **shot-window.** Perhaps a bow-window; perhaps a window that (opens and) shuts. This is one of the ballad-words that have been continued in tradition after the meaning has been forgotten; see Introduction, p. 8.

34. **yestreen** = yester e'en, yesterday evening.

44. **die**: see note on *Fair Annie of Rough Royal*, 110.

52. **lang or** = long ere, long before.

53. **done her**, betaken herself.

54. **Fa'n** = fallen.

59. This gives us a dramatic hint that the lady's father disapproved of her lover.

63. **gin** = if; **southin**, southern.

65. **till** = to.

66. **gar**, make, cause.

70. **deal**, distribute (as we say 'deal' of playing-cards).

73. **bigly** = lit. habitable; but as it is the 'stock epithet' of *bower*, it has lost part of its meaning. Cf. l. 101.

86. *i.e.* caused to be made for her a bier.

87—8. **tae...tither**; cf. **tone...tother** in *King Estmere*, 5—6.

90. **sark**, shroud.

100. **make** = mate, lover.

105. **sheave**, slice.

See also my *Popular Ballads*, First Series, 153.

THOMAS RYMER

'Thomas the Rhymer' is well-known from Sir Walter Scott's ballad in *The Minstrelsy of the Scottish Border*; his version is based on the one given here.

The ballad, in relating the journey of a mortal to the nether-world, must be associated with a vast number of popular stories of wide vogue, all of which relate such an incident. It is sufficient to suggest the visits of Odysseus to Hades and of Aeneas to the infernal regions. The story of Thomas is more closely connected with a legend of the Arthurian cycle, in which Morgan le Fay (an en-chantress, and King Arthur's sister) took Ogier the Dane away to live with her at Avalon for two hundred years, which seemed but twenty to Ogier.

Our ballad is the *débris* of a metrical romance, popular in the fifteenth century, called *Thomas of Erceldoune*. This romance tells first the story of Thomas's visit to 'fairyland,' and then proceeds to narrate how Thomas obtained from the Queen of Elfland his gift of prophecy.

For Thomas Rymour of Erceldoune is a historical character; he was a seer, poet, and prophet of the twelfth century, and 'prophecies' attributed to him were popular in Scotland until quite recently.

But we must suppose that some bard, between the twelfth and fifteenth centuries, wishing to put Thomas's prophecies into the form of a poem, thought it best to give first some explanation of his prophetic power; and, having elsewhere heard a good story about a visit to 'Elfland,' he tacked that story on to the tale of Thomas of Erceldoune. His prophecies, however, have entirely disappeared from the ballad; once again the ballad-singer is only concerned with the narrative.

7. **ilka**, each: **tett**, lock (of hair).

10. **till**, to.

11—14. This mistake on Thomas's part is paralleled by a similar mistake in the story referred to above, where Ogier the Dane mistakes Morgan le Fay for the Virgin.

20. **weal or wae**, weal or woe, good or ill.

44. **fairlies**, marvels, wonders.

50. **lily leven,** lily lawn, a smooth lawn set with lilies.

59. **gin ae,** if any.

61. **even cloth,** cloth with the nap or rough surface worn away.

See my *Popular Ballads*, Second Series, 1.

EDWARD

Compare this ballad with *Lord Randal.* As there, so here; *Edward* can be reduced to a simpler form in four-line stanzas:

> "Why does your brand sae drap wi' bluid,
> And why sae sad gang ye, O?"—
> "O, I hae killed my hauke sae guid,
> And I had nae mair but he, O."

Notice that it is *not absolutely necessary* to mention 'Edward' and his 'Mither' all through; if the ballad were recited in four-line stanzas as above, observe how much more *dramatic* the ending would be:

> "And what wul ye leive to your ain mother deir,
> My dear son, now tell me, O?"
> "The curse of hell frae me sall ye beir,
> Sic counseils ye gave to me, O."

—for until the word 'ye' in the last line, we should not know that it is his mother to whom the man is speaking. And we may suspect that the names have been added, as Edward occurs in no other Scottish ballad, except as the name of an English king.

13. **reid-roan** = red-roan, red or chestnut mixed with white or grey thickly interspersed.

16. **erst,** formerly.

20. **dule,** grief, pain, sorrow: **drie,** endure, undergo.

45. **The warldis room,** the space of the world, "the whole world wide." Otherwise we might read **The warld is room** = the world is wide, or spacious.

56. In this last line is a hint that the mother advised Edward to kill his father.

See also my *Popular Ballads*, First Series, 189.

THE TWA CORBIES

There is an English version, *The Three Ravens*, in a book published in 1611; but it does not approach the Scottish version in the beauty of its poetry.

2. **corbie**, the Scotch for *crow*.

5. **fail dyke**, wall of turf.

13. **hause-bane**, neck-bone, collar-bone.

16. **theek**, thatch.

THE BAILIFF'S DAUGHTER OF ISLINGTON

In many languages ballads are found, in which the simple plot is that a woman in disguise tells her lover that his sweetheart is dead, by way of trying his constancy.

"The Bailiff's Daughter of Islington" means the daughter of the bailiff of Islington. See note on *King Estmere*, 198.

The version given here is taken from a 'broadside' (see Introduction, pp. 2, 10).

12. *i.e.* to bind (him) an apprentice, to apprentice him to a trade. The usual period was seven years, as in line 13.

22. **puggish**, poor, ragged.

24. **require**, seek.

45—8. It is easy to rearrange the lines so as to rhyme, simply by transposing the second and third of this verse.

49—52. Notice that this verse appears to be added unnecessarily in the broadside version.

YOUNG BENJIE

The most interesting point about this ballad is its reference (ll. 53—60) to the custom of the 'lyke-wake,' concerning which there will be more to say in the notes to the next piece.

8. **plea**, quarrel.

13. **stout**, stiff, stubborn. See l. 37.

21. **burd**, maiden. See *Young Bekie*, 10.

27. **sets ye chuse,** befits you to choose.

30. **ee**=eyes.

36. **linn,** stream.

37, 38. **stout**: see note above, l. 13. Here it means she was resolute—not to be drowned, just as in the next line **laith to be dang**=loth to be dinged (beaten, overcome).

39. **wan**=won. Cf. note on *Fair Annie of Rough Royal*, 76.

40. **wan,** pale.

51. **ae,** only.

53. **lyke wake**=(literally) body-watch; the custom of watching the corpse of a dead person through the night. See notes on *The Lyke-wake Dirge. Lyke*, body, is the same word as *lych* in *lych-gate*, the covered gateway into a churchyard where a corpse is set down by the bearers of the bier.

Here we must notice that Marjorie's brothers have a reason for watching their sister's corpse, *because they suspect that she was murdered.* During the time between death and burial—that is, during the lyke-wake—the disembodied spirit is supposed to hover round the corpse, and will, if called upon, reveal the cause of death.

57. **Wi' doors ajar.** To leave the door 'partly open' was supposed to be a strong inducement to the dead to speak. Therefore it was usual either to shut it altogether, or to leave it wide open, because under ordinary circumstances the corpse was not desired to speak; the wide-open door was preferred, because the ceremony was attended by many neighbours and friends, and great hospitality was exhibited. Bodies are still so 'waked' in Ireland to-day.

candle-light: see *The Lyke-Wake Dirge*, 3.

59. **streikit**=stretched out.

60. **waked**=watched.

64. **thraw,** twist, turn.

67. **feared nae dout**: **dout**=fear. The phrase simply means 'had no fear.'

69. **ae**=one, or only. See above, note on 51.

73. **head,** *i.e.* behead.

81. **gravat,** cravat, neck-band. Benjie, it seems, was to be blinded, and then led about by a rope round his neck. But why should it be green?

87. **drie.** See note on *Edward*, 20.

88. **scug,** expiate, pay for.

THE LYKE-WAKE DIRGE

This song used to be sung during the watch over the body before burial. There is a version in a manuscript of 1686, where the song is recorded by a man who had it from his father sixty years previously; and the following note is attached.

"At the funerals in Yorkshire, to this day they continue the custom of watching and sitting up all night till the body is inhearsed. In the interim some kneel down and pray by the corpse, some play at cards, some drink and take tobacco; they have also mimical plays and sports....This belief in Yorkshire was, amongst the vulgar, and perhaps is in part still, that after the person's death the soul went over Whinny-moor."

The superstition as recorded in the *Dirge* is this: after death the spirit has to cross Whinny-moor (*i.e.* a moor covered with whins, or furze, and therefore prickly), the passage of which is facilitated by shoes; and the spirit of the man, who during his life charitably gave away even a single pair of shoes, is provided with that very pair to ease his way across the moor. Then comes the 'Brig o' Dread' (perhaps a corruption of the 'bridge of the dead,' or else = 'the dreadful bridge'), over which lies the way to Purgatory, where again those who were charitable in life reap their reward.

A superstition like this is not confined to Yorkshire, nor to England, nor even to Europe; ideas similar to those of the Bridge, the Moor, and the Shoes can be found in many lands and in all ages. Only a few can be given here. The early Scandinavian mythology contains all three; a bridge which rings to the tramp only of mortal feet; a moor over which all souls had to pass on their way to the realms of Hela, Goddess of Death; and *helsko*, Hell-shoon (or shoes), provided to assist the traveller. Another way of providing the dead with Hell-shoon is to burn a pair with the corpse; this superstition may be seen in a dialogue of Lucian, the Greek. Mohammedans have a belief that over their hell is stretched the *Al-Sirat*, a bridge finer than a hair and sharper than a razor.

Observe that in the *Dirge* this old, wide-spread, *Pagan* superstition is linked to a *Christian* refrain.

3. **Fire and fleet**: an expression formerly used in legal documents and wills, to mean 'fire and house-room'—two privileges that

a dying person might bequeathe. **Fleet** is actually the same word as the modern *flat* in the sense of a set of rooms in a house.

Another version of the *Dirge* reads 'Fire and sleet'; in which case *sleet* must be made to mean *salt*. In Scottish lyke-wakes a small wooden plate, containing a little salt, an emblem of the immortal spirit, and a little earth, carefully separated from the salt, to signify the corruptible body, was put on the breast of the corpse.

candle-light. A candle was invariably kept burning, throughout the lyke-wake, in the same room as the corpse.

9. **hosen and shoon**: notice the old plurals ending in *-n*; cf. *housen*, &c.

For this ballad and the last, see my *Popular Ballads*, Second Series, 83, 88, and Appendix, pp. 238—44.

THE DEMON LOVER

This ballad is unfortunately incomplete, there being a gap in the story after line 12. Fully narrated, it would run like this:—A woman, married to a ship's carpenter, but previously the sweetheart of another man who has since disappeared, is visited by a demon, who makes the woman believe it is her former lover. (In the missing portion the demon by some means tempts her away; perhaps she is fascinated by the idea of seeing "white lilies grow on the banks of Italie.") She leaves her husband and young son, goes on board the demon's ship, and is thrown into the sea and drowned.

16. **begane**, overlaid, decorated.

20. **alsua** = also (a Scottish spelling).

21. **haud**, hold.

28. **gurly**, tempestuous.

35—6. It is difficult to see the exact bearing of these lines on the story.

FAIR HELEN OF KIRCONNELL

This poem, it should be noticed, like others of these memorial-songs or dirges, is not exactly a narrative so much as a lyrical ballad. It appears, however, to be founded on the following traditional story.

Fair Helen, of the clan of Irving (or Bell), looked with favour on Adam Fleming; but her relatives pressed on her the suit of his rival, whose name is said to have been Bell (perhaps a kinsman). When

Helen continued to meet Adam in the kirkyard of Kirconnell, past which flows the river Kirtle, the jealous lover hid himself in the bushes on the bank; and, being discovered there by Helen, levelled his carbine at Adam. Helen flung herself into her true-love's arms and received the shot intended for him. Whereupon Adam slew his rival, and went abroad to Spain to fight infidels; but being still inconsolable returned and perished on Helen's grave. According to Sir Walter Scott, a tombstone with the inscription *Hic jacet Adamus Fleming* is to be seen (or was when Scott wrote) in the kirkyard of Kirconnell, which is near Dumfries.

The lament is supposed to be sung by Adam Fleming. The tune is still well-known.

7. **burd**: see *Young Bekie*, 10; *Young Benjie*, 21.

11. **meikle** = much. The phrase does not mean that Helen took great trouble to swoon; it means that she swooned as the result of much pain and trouble.

13—20. As these verses contain each only a pair of rhyming lines, it may be suspected that they have been dragged in from some other ballad of four lines to a verse. They are, moreover, a sudden change from lyric to narrative.

THE BONNY EARL OF MURRAY

James Stewart, son of Sir James Stewart of Doune (**Castle Down**, 22), became Earl of Murray by his marriage with the heiress of the Regent Murray, and was called bonny because he was "of comely personage, of a great stature, and strong of body like a kemp." In the last months of 1591, a rumour came to the King that Murray had either assisted in or countenanced the attack made a short time before on Holyrood House by Stewart, Earl of Bothwell; and Huntly was ordered to arrest him. Murray, however, refused to surrender to his feudal enemy Huntly, and the house of Donibristle—the Lady Doune's house, where Murray was—was set on fire. Murray rushed out, and was mortally wounded. There is a tradition that as he lay dying, Huntly struck him in the face, whereat the bonny Earl said, "You have spoiled a better face than your own." This took place in February, 1592.

Notice (from ll. 7—8) that this is the King's lament.

9. **braw**=brave.

10. **the ring** was a game of skill in horsemanship; the competitors attempting to thrust the point of a lance through a ring suspended by a cord from a beam.

18. It is not certain what kind of game **the glove** was.

BONNIE GEORGE CAMPBELL

Editors, who have wished to discover a historical foundation for this lament, have found plenty of George Campbells to whom it might refer. But another version gives the first name as James, so we need not attempt an exact definition.

10. **greeting**: see note on *Fair Annie of Rough Royal*, 70.

12. **rivin'**, tearing.

15. **toom**, empty.

17. The bonnie bride is supposed to be speaking.

19. *i.e.* My barn is still to be built.

THE TWA BROTHERS

In other versions of this ballad, the wound that Sir Willie gives Sir John is accidental. But this is a corruption, in all probability; it is far more characteristic of a ballad-hero that he should lose his temper and slay his brother. Moreover, the intentional murder adds to the pathetic generosity of the murdered brother in providing excuses for his absence to be made to his father, mother, and sister.

4. **warsle**=wrestle. The ballad, like many others, has become a children's game in certain parts of the world.

FAIR ANNIE

Fair Annie has been stolen from her home by a knight to become his bride, and they have seven sons. Apparently on account of his poverty, Lord Thomas, at the opening of the ballad, announces his intention of bringing home a richer bride, and Annie submits meekly. But it turns out that the new bride is Fair Annie's sister, so she returns home, leaving five rich ships behind her to relieve Lord Thomas.

2. **braw**, brave, handsome.

3. **gear**, goods, property.

S. 12

15. **jimp**. See *The Gardener*, 4.

16. **braid**, plait. This would make her appear to the new bride only a maiden, as married women wore their hair bound up, or under a cap. Customs of this kind are not yet extinct even in Great Britain.

55. **scoup**, fly, hasten.

57. **hang** = hanged.

64. **haud** = hold, keep, preserve.

81. **forbye**, apart. Cf. *Brown Adam*, 34.

91. **grew-hound** = greyhound.

95. **grat** = greeted, wept.

103. **girds** = girths, hoops.

116. **tyne**, lose.

See also my *Popular Ballads*, First Series, 29.

THE CRUEL BROTHER

The lesson in ancient etiquette that this ballad teaches is that it is unpardonable for a maiden not to secure her brother's consent to her marriage. In this story the brother was quite within his rights (in the eyes of the ballad's singer and audience) when he slew his sister.

Another characteristic point is that the dying girl should bequeathe good things to her friends (except 'sister Grace,' whose legacy is scarcely enviable), and evil things to her slayer and his wife. Compare similar testaments in *Edward*.

The refrain must of course be sung or recited in each verse.

2. **played o'er**, beat.

5. **mien**, face, appearance.

29. **close**, courtyard.

44. **pall**, robe.

56. **rive**, tear. See *Bonnie George Campbell*, 12.

YOUNG WATERS

Historical foundations have been elaborately sought for this ballad, but similar ballads are popular elsewhere; and the story is simple enough: a queen, by admiring a courtier too much, makes the king her husband jealous, and the courtier is put to death.

2. **round tables**, some kind of game, it is not known what.

13. **gowden-graith'd**, harnessed with gold.

41. This is the lament of Young Waters.

42. **but and** = and. Cf. *Young Bekie*, 31.

49. **heading-hill** = beheading-hill. Places of execution used to be selected on high ground, that the warning might be visible to many.

See also my *Popular Ballads*, First Series, 146.

BROWN ADAM

An excellent ballad, improving from verse to verse up to the last line, which contains a satisfactory climax.

6. **study** = stithy, anvil. This whole verse may be looked upon as an interpolation. Suspicion must always rest on verses in which the third line contains an internal rhyme, as here. Moreover, though ballads occasionally make extraordinary statements, no one can believe that a hammer of so soft a metal as gold could be of much use. Nor do smiths have white fingers, as a rule.

15. **biggit** = bigged, built. See *Bonnie George Campbell*, 19.

18. **thought lang**: see Introduction, p. 9, and *Young Bekie*, 64.

34. **forbye**, apart.

37. **he** is of course the full false knight.

41. **loo** = love.

46. **string**. Ancient purses were simply bags, the top being tied with a string.

51. **leman**, sweetheart.

KING EDWARD AND THE TANNER OF TAMWORTH

This Edward is called Edward IV. in the title of the ballad; but as similar stories are told not only of other Edwards and several Henrys, but also of kings other than English, it is simplest not to specify. The story of a king's encounter with a bluff yeoman appeals to the popular imagination in much the same way as a ballad of Robin Hood.

5. **bowne** = Scottish *boun*, ready.

16. It must be remembered that coins change in value according to the amount they will buy. As late as Elizabeth's reign, four shillings would buy what we now pay thirty or forty shillings for.

20. **weet**, know.

23. **readiest**, quickest, shortest.

29. **unready**, indirect.

43. **nobles**, coins worth one-third of a pound.

46. *i.e.*, and God send that you may enjoy (**prief**) them well.

48. The tanner thought the king to be a thief.

55. **unthrift**, spendthrift.

56. *i.e.*, you are surrounded by all you possess = you have no more than the clothes you stand up in.

67. **barker** = tanner. An infusion of bark is used in the process of tanning leather.

84. **boot**, payment.

86. **so mote I thee** = so may I thrive. A ballad 'commonplace,' used for strengthening an assertion.

94. **stound**, time.

97. **A groat** = 4*d*. (20 × 4*d*. = 6*s*. 8*d*., or a noble ; see l. 43).

110. **hilt**, flayed.

121—122. The tanner's 'cow-hide' was the *whole* skin, from horns to hoofs.

128. **brast** = burst, broken.

160. **lever** = rather; he would rather lose twenty pounds than be there.

161. The king calls for a collar to put on the tanner as a sign of knighthood; the tanner thinks he is going to be hanged.

175. **marks** are worth two nobles.

180. **Neat's-leather**, ox-leather. *Neat* = cattle; cf. *neat-herd*.

WILL STEWART AND JOHN

There is only one full text known of this ballad, and that is in the Percy Folio Manuscript (see Introduction, pp. 11—12); it displays as usual certain peculiarities of language (see notes on *The Lord of Learne*, 24, 42, &c.). The first verse in the MS. is apparently simply a lyrical introduction, and as it has nothing to do with the story, it is here omitted.

The ballad tells a capital story, but the allusions it contains to various old manners and customs make it interesting also from an antiquarian standpoint.

1. **by** = of, about.

5. **care-bed**: a bed to which a care-worn or troubled person used to go (cf. sick-bed). William, it will be seen, resorts to it often, always on account of his love (which he thinks is hopeless) for the Earl's daughter.

8. **that**: see note on *The Lord of Learne*, 24.

15—16. The relative 'whom' is dropped, and **her** inserted in its place.

24. **wight-men**, huntsmen. **cloth and fee**; clothing and money together formed the wages of servants of this kind.

26. **gone**=go (an old form of the infinitive).

32. **tydand**=tiding (another old form).

34. **could**=did: past tense of *can*, as in *King Estmere*, 273 (see note).

62. **meeten**=measured, *i.e.* a full mile; as one says 'a *good* mile.'

75. **ben**=are.

90. **rank**, sturdy, courageous.

108. **lope**=leapt.

116. **i-wis**, certainly. Cf. *The Lord of Learne*, 238.

134. See note above, l. 34.

136. **And-if**=if. See *King Estmere*, 148.

138. This, it should be observed, is the kiss of courtesy, which by ancient custom might be demanded by a knight of a lady.

140. **teemed**, allowed.

141—144. These **games** were football-matches, which were always popular on the Scottish Border. Sir Walter Scott notes that such games were the means of collecting large bodies of men together— sometimes with evil result, as on one occasion at least a murder was plotted at a grand football meeting.

163. **And**=if.

168. **Thou 'st**=thou shalt. Cf. *The Lord of Learne*, 130.

174. **chamber**, restrain, suppress.

191. **plewed**. This word is unknown; the meaning must be guessed.

195. **cordevain**: see note on *The Lord of Learne*, 91.

199. **room**, place, position.

205. **the King his**=the King's. See note on *King Estmere*, 198.

237. Notice this description of the beggar's dress, and of his equipment in l. 308. **clouted**, patched.

243. **stoutest**, bravest.

252. **buttery**, store-room.

258. **the dole-day**: *i.e.* the day when the great houses gave away *doles* (cf. *deal*, to give out—a word we still use in games of cards; cf. *The Gay Goshawk*, 70), or gifts of food, drink and money.

265. **dealt**: see last note.

275. **avale**, take off. Lit. 'lower,' of the visor of a helmet.

290. **witting**, knowing, aware.

292. *i.e.* by the time the sun has travelled a quarter of his journey.

307. **showing horn** is supposed to mean *shoeing-horn*, as a pun on the beggar's horn, as it might assist him in taking in his liquor. For **bag** cf. *The Heir of Linne*, 75.

336. **barne**=bairn, child.

337. **thee** is John Stewart. The Earl of Mar is of course indignant that his daughter should have been carried off; but his indignation does not prevent him from making a pun on his own name in l. 340.

BEWICK AND GRAHAME

In this ballad we are more definitely on the Border than in the last, and the next three are true 'Border Ballads.' A feature of this ballad is the allusion to the old institution of 'brotherhood in arms' (l. 56; cf. also the use of *bully*=brother). The tragical conclusion points a moral, that fathers, even if merry with wine, should not boast about the respective merits of their sons.

18. **bully**=brother. (So in Scottish *minnie*=mother, *tittie*=sister.) **bully** is the same word as *billie* in *Dick o' the Cow*, 6. It is used by Shakespeare of Bottom the weaver in the *Midsummer-Night's Dream*.

44. **by**=on account of. Compare *by* in *Will Stewart and John*, 1.

57. **limmer loon**: lit., low-born wretch.

85. **plate-jack**, plated coat.

94. **belive**, soon.

102. **farleys**, strange things. Cf. *fairlies* in *Thomas Rymer*, 44.

114. *i.e.* let me be free of thy brotherhood. Compare lines 126, 130, &c.

151—2. He vaulted over the fence. **lap**=lope, as in *Will Stewart and John*, 108.

169. **ackward.** Perhaps 'back-handed,' perhaps simply 'awk-ward.'

177. **horse,** get on horse-back. Bewick means 'ride away.'

189. **moudie-hill,** mole-hill. We must of course understand that he stuck the pommel of his sword in the soft earth, with the point upwards.

214. **block**=bargain: *i.e.* 'I have had the worst of the bargain.'

See also my *Popular Ballads*, Third Series, 101.

DICK O' THE COW

This and the following ballad are concerned with the raiders and 'cattle-lifters' (cattle-thieves) of the Border, who flourished about the middle of the sixteenth century. The Armstrong family were always prominent in these affairs, which as a rule take place in or near Liddesdale, a valley on the Scottish side of the Border, just to the north of Carlisle.

'Dick o' the Cow' does not mean 'Dick of the Cattle,' because the word in Scotch would be 'Kye.' 'Cow' perhaps means 'broom,' implying that Dick lived in a hut built in the broom or furze.

1. **lain in :** *i.e.* not gone out 'riding.'

3. **lidder,** lazy.

6. **billie,** brother. See *Bewick and Grahame*, 18.

7. **feed**=feud.

18. **know,** hillock, a low rise.

32. Cf. *Bewick and Grahame*, 114.

46. **leal,** loyal.

54. **Hairibie,** the place of execution at Carlisle.

57. **at,** of.

62. **drie,** endure, hold out. See *Edward*, 20, &c.

73. **plain**=complain.

74. **syne,** as well, also.

79—80. *i.e.* we'll tie him up in the sheet by the four corners, give him all the blows he can bear, and let him go.

84. **hough,** ankle, joint of the foot.

86. **dought,** was able.

92. **mense,** house.

97. **aevery,** ravenous.

103. **St Mary knot,** a triple knot.

118. **leal**, true. Cf. l. 46.
129. **jack**, jerkin, coat.
130. **leugh**, low.
140. **mo**, more.
157. **or**=ere, before: **blan**, stopped.
160. **plummet**, pommel, handle.
185. **gart**=garred, made.
200. **tell'd**=told, counted out.
223. **and**=if. See l. 240.
237. **lap a loup**=leapt a leap.
238. **leugh**=laughed.
240. **and**=if.
252. All the places in this ballad, except **Burgh under Stanemuir** are round Liddesdale. See the map in my *Popular Ballads*, Third Series.

JOHN O' THE SIDE

More than most, this ballad plunges into its subject, narrating in the first two lines that John o' the Side (which is on the river Liddel in Liddesdale, nearly opposite Mangerton) is taken prisoner for having slain Peter o' Whitfield. Peter appears also in another ballad, not so good as this, which is called *Hobby Noble* after its hero, whose acquaintance we make in this ballad.

John o' the Side was another of the Armstrong family, the famous freebooters, and first appears about 1550 in a list of borderers against whom complaints were laid before the Bishop of Carlisle.

This text of the ballad, from the Percy Folio MS., is much better than that inserted in *The Minstrelsy of the Scottish Border* by Sir Walter Scott. The ninth line, which can be guessed fairly easily, is missing in the MS.

5. **Sybil** is John's mother, as is shown by l. 78.
28. **Tyvidale**=Teviotdale, north of Liddesdale, in Roxburgh.
32. **badgers**, pedlars, corn-dealers, carrying bags.
37. **Culerton**, Chollerton, on the Tyne.
44. **gate**, way.
46. Cf. *The Lord of Learne*, 122 and note.
52. **tree**, wood.
59. **well-good** is simply a stronger form of 'good.'
72. **where as**=where.

80. **woe** = woeful.

103. **bastard-brother**, a half-brother.

110. **till** = to.

112. **tent**, guard; **gelding**, a horse, as in *The Lord of Learne*, 266.

125. **Flanders files**. It is not known that files were specially made in Flanders; but, whatever they were, they appear to have been useful and highly effective.

132. Because his legs were chained.

137. **lough**, laughed. See note on *Dick o' the Cow*, 238.

141. **thorough** = through. The old form of the word survives in a few words, such as *thoroughfare, thoroughbred*, &c.

160. **fain**, pleasure.

SIR HUGH IN THE GRIME

This ballad, of which the text here given is from a 'broadside' (see Introduction, pp. 2, 10), exhibits a curious corruption in the hero's name. 'Hugh in the Grime' = Hugh of the Graeme (Graham), or, simply, Hugh Graham.

The full story is not given in this ballad; Sir Hugh was hanged at Carlisle because he stole the bishop's mare—so much we learn. But Sir Hugh's theft of the mare was only a retaliation for a more serious wrong, said to have been done to him by the bishop. Whether the charge is true or not, sympathy is enlisted on behalf of Sir Hugh as against the Bishop of Carlisle; and Hugh Graham may have been on the same list as John o' the Side (see note on last ballad).

1. **Lord John** of this ballad is Lord Scroop, Warden of the West-Marches (on the Border), who appears in *Kinmont Willie*.

21. **good Lady Ward** and **Lady Moor** (33) have not been identified.

56. **fee**, reward. Compare *The Lord of Learne*, 221, &c.

For these last three Border Ballads, see also my *Popular Ballads*, Third Series, 75, 156, and 89.

THE BRAES OF YARROW

Yarrow Water is a tributary of the Tweed, and flows into it near Abbotsford, Sir Walter Scott's house.

The ballad tells us that a man, married to a lady with nine brothers, was considered by them to be an 'unmeet marrow' (*i.e.* an unfit mate) for her; so in true ballad style they slew him, though he killed four of them.

25. **dowy**, dark, gloomy; **den**, valley.

27. **well-wight**, strong, sturdy.

42. **dule**, grief. We must suppose that if the dule and sorrow was shown by Douglas, he was trying to pretend that he had not assisted in the murder. It is possible, however, within the limits of ballad-grammar, to understand that it was the sister who was grieved.

53. **kaimed**, combed.

58. **side**, long.

59. **hause-bane**, neck. Cf. *The Twa Corbies*, 13.

60. **tint**, ended.

SIR PATRICK SPENCE

This version of a famous ballad simply narrates that 'the king' chose Sir Patrick Spence, as his best sailor, to sail his ship; we are not told what the cargo was, nor whither the ship was bound. 'Dumferling' (Dunfermline) is on the north side of the Firth of Forth; and if 'haf owre to Aberdour' means merely half-way across the Firth from Aberdour (near Dunfermline), Sir Patrick's voyage was not a long one.

Later versions of the ballad, however, contain other details. The ship is bound for Norway, and the freight is a king's daughter. In one case the object of the voyage is to bring back the king of Norway's daughter; in another, to bring home the king of Scotland's daughter; or again, to take the Scottish king's daughter out to Norway. In support of the last variation of the story, it has been discovered that Margaret, daughter of Alexander III. of Scotland, was married to Erik, king of Norway, in 1281; and many of the knights who accompanied her to Norway were drowned in a storm— but on the *return* voyage. Those who attempt to prove our ballad historical, in accordance with these facts, also point out that 'half over to Aberdour' (*i.e.* from Norway) is a small island called Papa Stronsay, on which there is a tumulus known as 'the Earl's knowe' (knoll), and this is said to mark the grave of Sir Patrick Spence. The ballad may have been founded on fact, but it is idle to speculate.

Sir Walter Scott's version of this ballad is unnecessarily long. He calls the hero Spens.

5. **eldern**, elderly, old.

6. Notice omission of the relative; also l. 12.

9. **braid**, broad (a ballad-commonplace).

13—16. This usually happens when ballad-people receive letters. Compare *The Lord of Learne*, 337–340.

22. **the morne**=in the morning, to-morrow.

25—26. When the crescent moon appears to hold in its curve the rest of the globe, dimly visible, it is regarded as an omen of bad weather.

29. **laith**, loth.

30. **weet**=wet. Shoes at one time were made with heels of cork.

32. **they** refers to **hats**; **aboone**=above. The nobles' hats swam on the surface, above the nobles.

35. **Or ere**=before. See *Young Bekie*, 43; *The Gay Goshawk*, 52; &c.

41. **Haf owre**=half (way) over. See above.

42. **fadom**=fathom; as *fader*=father, in *Edward*, 21.

THE GARDENER

This pretty little ballad is characteristic in that it is a lyrical dialogue, in which the lady retorts in riddling fashion on her lover, refusing his suit. In the course of its existence it has become confused with other folk-songs of the same kind.

I have supplied two missing lines (27, 28).

3. **leal** (lit. loyal), true.

4. **jimp**, slender. Cf. *Fair Annie of Rough Royal*, 3.

5. **fancy**, like, desire. The word is still used in this sense.

8. **weed**, dress. Cf. *King Estmere*, 32.

10. The relative *which* is probably omitted here.

11. **jellyflower**=gilliflower, pink.

14. **camovine**=camomile.

17. **kail-blade**, the leaf of some vegetable, perhaps lettuce.

19. **coot**, ankle.

20. **brawn** (*i.e.* muscle of the leg), calf.

23. **blaewort**, the blue cornflower.

THOMAS O' POTT

The hero of this ballad is the serving-man's ideal—a menial successful in marrying a nobleman's daughter. It is probably not much earlier than the seventeenth century, quite late for a ballad; and this version comes from the Percy Folio.

1. The first verse is a kind of invocation.

2. **blee**, countenance.

12. **she 'st**=she shall. Cf. ll. 16, 62, &c.

25. **Gif**=if. Cf. *gin*, *The Gay Goshawk*, 63.

44. *i.e.*, the lady is betrothed to Lord Phenix.

54. **thereas**=whereas (see *John o' the Side*, 72), where.

68. *i.e.*, 'I will have no more to do with him.'

69. **that.** See note, *The Lord of Learne*, 24.

78. See note on *Sir Patrick Spence*, 13—16.

86. *i.e.*, So it shall be proved by her promise.

88. **Without**=unless. Still so used.

130. **doubt**, fear.

138. **row**, roll; as we say 'rolling in riches.'

160. **bride** does not imply that Lady Rosamond was the wife of Lord Phenix. See above, l. 44, and below, l. 190.

171. **an outside**, a quiet or retired spot.

191. **lough**=laughed. See *John o' the Side*, 137, &c.

192. **fain**, happy.

224. **angels**, pieces of money. The expression means 'throw away money,' or as we say now 'play ducks and drakes with it.'

230. **fain**, desirous. Compare l. 192, and see *The Lord of Learne*, 76.

232. *i.e.*, How shall I pay you back?

238. **rank**, high-fed. Compare *Will Stewart and John*, 90.

249. **ben**=are.

250. *i.e.*, are but little acquainted with the training that older horses have undergone.

291. **stiff and stout.** Probably a corruption of *stiff in stour*, for which see *King Estmere*, 272.

304.   He used one of the many charms that are popularly supposed to stop bleeding.   Samuel Pepys records a Latin one in his Diary:

> "Sanguis mane in te,
> Sicut Christus fuit in se;
> Sanguis mane in tua vena,
> Sicut Christus in sua poena;
> Sanguis mane fixus,
> Sicut Christus quando fuit crucifixus."

318.   **Sith** = since.

350.   **nigh**, approach.   Cf. *King Estmere*, 218.

For EU product safety concerns, contact us at Calle de José Abascal, 56–1°, 28003 Madrid, Spain or eugpsr@cambridge.org.

www.ingramcontent.com/pod-product-compliance
Ingram Content Group UK Ltd.
Pitfield, Milton Keynes, MK11 3LW, UK
UKHW020316140625
459647UK00018B/1896